THE BUSINESS GUIDE TO PROFITABLE CUSTOMER RELATIONS

THE BUSINESS GUIDE TO PROFITABLE CUSTOMER RELATIONS
Today's techniques for success

Jacqueline Dunckel
Brian Taylor

Self-Counsel Press
(*a division of*)
International Self-Counsel Press Ltd.
Vancouver
Toronto   Seattle

Printed in Canada

First edition: November, 1988

Canadian Cataloguing in Publication Data

Dunckel, Jacqueline, 1930-
The business guide to profitable customer relations

(Self-counsel series)
ISBN 0-88908-684-2
1. Customer relations. I. Taylor, Brian, 1931-
II. Title. III. Series.
HF5415.D85   1988   658.'12   C88-091462-9

Self-Counsel Press
(*a division of*)
International Self-Counsel Press Ltd.
1481 Charlotte Road
North Vancouver, British Columbia, V7J 1H1

CONTENTS

LIST OF FIGURES

LIST OF SAMPLES

INTRODUCTION

This is a down-to-earth book. There is no learned treatise within — just clear and effective talk on why businesses that ignore customer relations do so at their peril.

We'll discuss how successful major organizations devote considerable resources to reading public attitudes and perceptions, *why* they believe a customer relations strategy is a crucial part of their business strategy, *what* they see as the benefits, *where* and *when* they build customer service into their planning process, and *how* you can do the same for your business — large or small.

We'll talk about three questions and the answers that could keep you in business. The first: What is "bad" customer relations? The second: What is "good" customer relations? And the third question: How can I improve the current customer relations of my business?

You'll also find plans and programs in the following pages that have worked successfully for others. With a little bit of ingenuity and adaptation, they could work equally well for you or your organization.

If you're serious about beefing up the bottom line of your business, then the advice in this book will get you headed in the right direction and then keep you on target. More important, you will understand why customer service is moving up the priority list in dynamic companies and why it is consuming more of their time and budget.

So let's start with a brief survey. Ask people why they patronize a particular business or retail store and chances are good that they will say it's because there is a good product, good service, convenient location, or any one of a variety of complimentary comments. Chances are also good they will *not* say it's because they practice good customer relations.

It's ironic that when an establishment is recognized as outstanding in the business community, seldom do we think that the image it projects is planned. Yet very few organizations enjoy a favorable image by luck. Public goodwill comes from a good performance that is sensibly planned, carefully executed, and publicly acknowledged. It is earned, not bestowed.

In the past, it was common for someone in business to think that "if I'm good at my business, providing good service and quality products, I'll be successful. Word will automatically spread." Well, perhaps it may spread — but probably not far enough or fast enough to keep up with the changing tastes and preferences of today's society.

Granted, you need good service and quality products to first attract the customers. But you must retain their interest to maintain your relationship. You do this by letting them know you care. While you let them know the material benefits they gain from you are substantial, you must also, psychologically and subliminally, let them know you recognize them as an important and worthwhile part of your business. People crave recognition. Cater to that need and you will be successful. Consider your clients and customers as part of your extended family.

Equally important is letting potential clients and future customers know that they, too, can become a part of your "family" and receive the same courtesy and consideration, in addition to the same dedicated services, you afford your present clientele.

Now, much of this may sound familiar, particularly if you've been involved in public relations or community relations, and much of it is similar — particularly the guiding principles. But differences may arise in the methods of implementing plans or programs.

Using the prerogative of artistic license, we've drawn a parallel between customer service and public relations in this quotation attributed to *Fortune Magazine* by substituting "customer service" for "public relations:" "Good [customer service] is good performance — publicly appreciated."

Doesn't that sentence sum up the essence of what customer service is all about? While it may seem self-evident to spread the word about your good deeds, tragically too often people let opportunity dribble through their fingers. You must make the most of each opportunity, seizing it as though it were your last, and exploiting it to its fullest advantage.

In the *Fortune Magazine* quotation, "good performance" comes before "publicly appreciated." This is no accident of the pen. You cannot expect clients or customers to thank you or express appreciation for something they haven't yet received, no matter how noble your intent or glittering the promise.

All the exotic plans, goals, and objectives in the world don't mean a thing while they remain as plans, goals, and objectives. It is when you put them into practice that they begin to have relevance and meaning. Many businesses have floundered on the rocks of procrastination — despite thoughtful planning and meticulous strategy — because the plans remained on paper. Nobody was committed to them. This is often the pivotal point of customer service. Frequently, the commitment to transform plans and promises into reality fades under pressure of day-to-day business activity. Yet an organization without a sensible, comprehensive, and active service philosophy is living on borrowed time.

Abraham Lincoln prophesied wisely and well when he said, "With public sentiment nothing can fail; without it, nothing can succeed." Over a century ago, Lincoln recognized that public opinion, sentiment, or perception is a powerful and motivating force in society. Today it remains just as powerful and influential in society but has also migrated into our business economy.

Wise business people accept customer service as an essential element in public opinion. It is also a powerful management tool. When used well, it returns dividends far beyond the initial outlay of funds or investment in time and energy.

Business leaders also recognize that good customer service is not an emergency response to a crisis or a stopgap measure to bolster sagging sales. It isn't something you can get into and out of as the mood grips you or as circumstances dictate. Rather it is an ongoing, credible, and planned business activity with significant support from senior management.

So what do you need to establish or enhance a customer service program in your business? Simple. You need to think about customer service. You need to fantasize, visualize, and then realize. You need to eat, drink, and sleep it. Then you need to plan it, develop it, provide it, launch it, sustain it, encourage it, and, finally, be thankful for it — because it's paying your salary. Moreover, you must sell it to your employees because it pays their salaries as well.

If you agree with what we have said so far, read on, and we will tell you what is needed to start a vigorous customer service program, plus we will tell you who should be involved, why they need to be involved, and why their cooperation is essential to your success.

1
CUSTOMER SERVICE — WHAT IT IS AND WHAT IT IS NOT

Ask most people what customer service is and they will tell you what it is not. We all have stories of long lineups, rude waiters, indifferent clerks, lost luggage, and service technicians on interminable coffee breaks.

Many can recall, with blissful nostalgia, what service used to be. Back in the forties and fifties, when labor was cheap and prices stable, your milk arrived at the door every morning at the same time. You could phone the drugstore and have a prescription delivered free of charge, often by the druggist personally. You knew your bank manager's name and the manager knew yours. When you went to fill your car with gas, you stayed in the car, the tank was filled, the windows washed, and the oil checked by a band of uniformed gas attendants. Every Saturday you checked out the latest 45s at the music store with its individual booths where you could play the record before buying it. It was definitely an era of service.

a. WHAT IS CUSTOMER SERVICE?

So what is customer service and what happened to it? Customer service, or good customer relations, can be described as expectations:

- The expectation that a product will produce the benefits promised.

- The expectation that the service will be of the standard promised.

- If expectations are not met, the seller will make good on the promise.

Good customer relations is a continuing, mutually satisfying contract between two economic entities.

b. THE CHANGE IN FRONTLINE STAFF

When our economy was blue collar based and those in the service industry were in the minority, good service was more easily measured and taken for granted. A person's word was a bond, and a handshake as good as a contract. By the mid-fifties, white collar workers in technical, managerial, and clerical jobs outnumbered blue collar workers. Still, good customer service was expected and it was delivered. By the seventies, inflation caused businesses to slash services to keep prices down. Deregulation led to price wars and cutbacks. A good example of this occurred in the transportation systems industry, particularly in the United States. Management moved behind closed doors. It became difficult to hire frontline service workers because of labor shortages, and the attitude toward service jobs deteriorated.

Another common example of deteriorating service is the restaurant industry. Think back; when did you last meet a "waiter"? Usually, waiters are either actors "at liberty" or students working toward their MBAs. In contrast, throughout Europe there is pride in being a waiter. It is considered a profession that takes time to master, and, as a result, the service provided is generally much better than in North America.

The final, and very important, factor that has contributed to the decline in customer service in recent years is that human workers have been replaced with computers and the self-service concept. Today, as a result of the reduction in services and increased automation to save money, consumers find themselves doing business with frontline people who are underpaid, undertrained, and undermotivated. They are overworked to keep labor costs down and underpaid to keep product prices down. They are unmotivated because they see no future with the company. How can they develop a sense of pride if they find it difficult to experience a sense of accomplishment? Treated as the lowest people on the ladder, working in jobs that emphasize skills that require little training, they are not expected to solve the customer's problems or be creative. The frontline worker has become a human robot with no decision-making responsibility. Even the standardized greetings — "Hi, I'm Ned. I'll be serving you this evening" — and the inevitable "Have a nice day!" have no warmth, personality, or meaning.

The customer's concerns or feelings take second place at best. In most large department stores today, shopping is a jungle experience of searching through over-stocked counters and back-to-back racks. Waiting on yourself, you search for the cashier's enclave, wait in line, then wait some more as the cashier taps a multi-digit inventory code into the computer. You are lucky if you make eye contact.

c. THE CHANGING DEMANDS OF THE CUSTOMER

Where once the customer was king, he or she now seems to be barely tolerated. "If only the customers would go away and leave me alone, I could get my work done," was heard from a travel agent. "This would be a great job if it weren't for the students," from a college admissions clerk. "These elevator managers make such demands," from a supervisor at a grain purchasing company.

In these cases, the work has become more important than the travelers seeking information, the students, and the grain buyers who are responsible in the first place for there being any work and, consequently, any pay. The machinery and the system has taken precedence. We have become obsessed with servicing the job rather than the customer.

Customers have tolerated this situation for some time. Eighty-seven percent of the public gave up service in hope of lower prices. For awhile, everyone shopped at mega-bulk stores, filled their own tires, and made lonely treks to the bank machines. But by the time the 1980s rolled around, two-income families were more common; as a result, time and schedules became even more important. Now the public wants convenience plus quick, personal service. Minor inconveniences fray a customer's nerves and lead to vocal demands.

Once again, consumers are saying "help me" and meaning it. It is not a plea; it is a demand. Since 60% of North American industries are service industries, consumers now have the luxury of being able to shop around for that help, whether it be for transportation, communication, utilities, financial consultation, insurance, real estate, accounting, food, clothing, recreation, or personal needs. Consumers are returning to those companies who always knew what their customers wanted or anticipated what they would want. Whenever people travel, they can be sure that MacDonalds will provide the same burger, served in clean surroundings, and delivered quickly; IBM will have the "future" machine developed today; Woodwards, a western Canadian department store, really means it when they say, "The customer is always right," and the Central Coffee Shoppe in the southern U.S. town of Manning, which has had a member of the Metropole family behind the counter for over 50 years, still serves the wonderful lemon pie that kept actor Jimmy Cagney returning again and again.

d. YOUR BUSINESS AND THE FUTURE OF CUSTOMER SERVICE

You will have a distinct competitive edge going into the 1990s if you, your company, or organization recognize that service — good customer relations — is not just the business of frontline employees, but the business of everyone. Everyone

4

will have to recognize that it is a tool you have to budget for, train to use, and most important, believe in its value.

While each marketplace is different in size, scope, and magnitude, all marketplaces, all vendors and stall holders in the market, and all market frequenters operate under the principle of "presumed satisfaction," or "assumed response." For example, if you buy a can opener, you expect it to work. If not, you expect the store to give you another, return your money, or have the faulty one repaired. Today, this is the hidden message on all items in the market. Maybe you didn't put that message on your goods and services and maybe you don't believe it is there because you can't actually see it. But, rest assured, it *is* there.

It is not the message itself that can play havoc with your organization, it is your response to that implied message that can dislodge the fulcrum and upset the balance. That is what we zero in on in this book: blending the ingredients in the marketplace. Instead of rehashing all the motherhood statements about excellence that have been made over the past few years, which we presume you agree with as we do, we want to clear the decks and get down to some basic ideas. We believe you want techniques and suggestions to build a quality service program in your company. So let's plan it together.

2
THE "WHY" OF CUSTOMER RELATIONS

Probably the first thought that entered your mind when you picked up this book was "I hope it's not just another get better-richer-faster text that shows how to eliminate stress while hugging your boss and reducing carbohydrate intake." In other words, satisfaction in 17 seconds a day.

If that is what you are expecting, return this book to the shelf and wend your way back to your office because there is no magic in these pages. Instead, this book will focus on, and help you focus on, the reality of the marketplace. Once you accept that the market is the great determinant, the fulcrum on which your entire future pivots, then you can get down to the business of good business, which is servicing the people with whom you would like to do business.

a. THE 90-SECOND TEST

Before you saddle up and ride off in all directions, ask yourself three very basic questions about improvement in service excellence and about your organization. Allow yourself 30 seconds to answer each question.

(a) Why us? (What do we stand to gain?)

(b) Why now? (What could we gain from a delay?)

(c) Why bother? (What do we stand to lose?)

These are excellent questions to kick off your mental process.

As an active participant in the business world, whether entrepreneur or employee, you are operating in a marketplace of wants and needs, goods and services, nourished by a constant stream of demands. Each vendor in the marketplace has a stall stuffed with people and products, in all shapes and sizes, for your selection. The products are attractively packaged and the ribbon and tinsel tend to draw your eyes away from the unobtrusive security tag that represents expectations.

Most people pay little attention to the electronic message on the security tags on products in a department store, unless they happen to walk through the exit without paying for an item. Then, ringing alarms announce the oversight to everyone within five blocks. The department store has expectations that most people will pay for their selections. From experience, they also know that some people will not, so they condition customers, by the use of the security system, to realize that everyone has a responsibility for his or her actions.

Business is much the same. All actions come with expectation tags either real or imagined. Customers expect business to respond to their demands. How well business people respond to customer expectations determines how long they remain in business. If the expectations are met (i.e., paid for), the alarm stays silent. If not, the alarm tolls ominously.

1. Why us?

As you think about why you should implement a customer relations plan, keep in mind that whether you know it or not, you already have a program in place, although it may be informal or invisible, and that program definitely says something about your business. Think about the last complaint you received about you, your company, or about your employees and their interaction with the public. Was it very recent? For the sake of comparison, try to recall the last time you received a compliment, and mentally weigh the number of complaints against the number of compliments. If complaints are outnumbering compliments, ask yourself if your business is unknowingly implementing a poor customer relations program.

While it is accepted that people complain more readily than they compliment, there is always a definite reason for both actions — a cause and effect. Complaints can be real, imagined, or perceived. They can be implied or intangible, but in the mind of the victim they are always very real and can often block out other more important matters. Whatever category the complaint falls into, there is a direct correlation to the bottom line. Dissatisfied customers or clients have an impact on profits, which is the most sensitive area in business.

One word of warning: some people think in terms of the "quick fix" as a substitute for service excellence and our advice is "don't do it!" In the long run, it won't work, and it often doesn't work in the short term, either.

Temporary patch jobs, while they take on the air of permanence, never get better because they are built on a makeshift foundation. An ad hoc solution may get an angry client off the phone or off your back, but the phone will certainly ring again when the "patch" peels off.

Some companies grasp for the quick fix and plan to initiate programs of good customer relations and service excellence when times get better and finances aren't so tight. But it is essential to accept that service excellence isn't a "good times" or even a part-time exercise. It must be a continual and consistent process. The old adage "an ounce of prevention is worth a pound of cure" is still true today. You have to make the time available to implement a permanent customer relations program because it is becoming increasingly more evident that satisfying the expectations for quality in products and services is the key to survival for many businesses.

2. Why now?

The second question, why now?, is harder to answer. Who really knows when an appropriate time really is appropriate? Like most business decisions, the answer to this question is based on informed intuition. But here is a rule of thumb for customer relations: If you don't have a program in place, in the works, or in the back of your mind, the best time for you and your company is right now!

Even if you have had a program running for several years, now may be the time to evaluate the results, examine the original objective, and see if your goals and results are still valid. Time may have burnished them, but more than likely it has tarnished them. Perhaps it's time for reassessment and/or rededication to the principles you enunciated at an earlier time. That old phrase, "it's never too early, but it could be too late," still holds true.

3. Why bother?

Why bother? is a key question, and should be asked more often about everything you do. It is easier to assume that a good reason to get involved exists rather than making the time to thoroughly check whether your involvement has relevance to the goals of the organization and the needs of your public.

We mentioned earlier that society is changing substantially. Every area in which humans operate today comes under public scrutiny — not a casual glance but intensive investigation under a microscope. Business and industry is being challenged like never before, and respected business leaders familiar with traditional corporate activities now find themselves thrust into a public arena where they must defend their policies and corporate actions. It is a way of life that many find difficult and is exacerbated as time-honored standards are rejected by questioning publics and consumers.

When you tie this together with quickly evolving scientific and technical advances, a bewildered, and often hostile, audience responds by lashing out at the handiest large target — the omnipresent corporation. It is no accident that individuals are willing to tackle the "Goliaths" in business and industry. For some it takes on the flavor of a crusade, a battle of the small guy against overwhelming odds in money and materials. Poor David gains the sympathy of the public, frequently the politicians, and sometimes the judiciary, who more and more are looking at the issue of "expectations."

Where are the "Davids" of the world gaining victories? Quite often it is in insignificant battles about rights: the right to know, the right of common sense. For example, the small print in legal documents or insurance policies is being questioned and is often tainted as an escape route for business in sticky situations. These documents are written in legal jargon that leaves a reader befuddled, and usually another lawyer has to be employed to interpret both meaning and intent.

These changing values in society provide challenges, but they also provide opportunities to enhance conditions and perceptions for growth and, ultimately, profit. Good customer relations pays off. It fosters loyalty and productivity with employees, encourages pride in accomplishment, attracts the capable people you need to operate successfully, and, most important, creates respect and goodwill with customers, clients, suppliers, government representatives, and your community. In doing this, it also creates a continuing demand for your organization's services, which means your business can grow, and so can you as an individual.

b. CAN IT WORK FOR YOU?

While we use the term survival to describe the reasons for customer service, perhaps it is more palatable to think of it as "enlightened self-interest." And if you are talking about self-interest, doesn't it make sense to become involved in your own destiny? You can no longer abdicate your future to chance, or to the "I'll get around to it" philosophy of an individual who has been "volunteered" to develop and implement the program, and who may already be swamped with major responsibilities.

Just as you have your personal priorities, so, too, must your business. We believe that if survival is part of your company's plans for the future, then quality, service, and excellence need to be boosted higher on the list of priorities.

Can it be done? Most certainly. It starts with commitment — to yourself, to your company and to your plan. You need to become committed to setting standards, designing a strategy, developing plans, and then implementing them. These are the four simple but crucial steps to survival in today's business market.

c. CHECKING OUT ATTITUDES

Next time you are in a store, try this simple exercise. It may reinforce an attitude you have about the store, or it may change your attitude entirely.

Choose an item in the store, and then ask a clerk if it is available in another color, style, or model. If so, ask how much it would cost, and how long before it would come in. Then see how much time the clerk is willing to devote to answering your questions and making you feel your request is important. Does the clerk respond well to you? Does he or she display an attitude of interest, of caring about satisfying you? Is he or she courteous, diplomatic, and anxious to please?

This same scenario is played out daily around the world in literally billions of transactions, and each one is an opportunity to improve or cement a relationship, each one is a chance to ensure survival. Make a commitment to grasp all of those opportunities for your company. Do you know how your customers are treated by your staff? Do you encourage good customer relations?

d. THE KEY WORD IS IMPROVEMENT

We said earlier there is no magic solution in this book that can make problems evaporate, and as a business person you already know that. You are probably skeptical about getting richer-better-faster for some very good reasons.

But we do have to emphasize that getting better is central to any strategy to improving quality and service. It is fundamental to business and industry as well as to the individual because there is a built-in need to improve; it's part of our nature — our psyche. We are all born strivers and achievers, whether we like it or not. Where we differ is the level of achievement we are satisfied with, and that depends on the goals we set for ourselves, and the goals we expect to accomplish.

Trying to get better also allows you to look back at former accomplishments, gauge your improvement, and set higher and more demanding benchmarks of satisfaction. This is what happened at The ABC Shoppe, the store in the case study that will be examined at the end of each section of this book. By following this case study, you will experience first hand the procedures we suggest in this book that can then be transferred to your own company or situation.

CASE STUDY: THE ABC SHOPPE — A GIFT BOUTIQUE FOR MEN AND WOMEN

After careful market research, a freelance writer, John, and a dentist, Mary, have opened a specialty boutique that sells upgrade accessories for men and women. They are adequately financed and located in a trendy area near other stores of equal quality. Their stock features shirts, blouses, ties, socks, sweaters, scarves, jewelry, and travel and gift items.

John is able to give more time to the store, so he has assumed the role of manager. Mary, who has an active dental practice, takes over the bookkeeping and buying chores. She travels a great deal, which makes it possible for her to visit markets and make personal selections for the store.

John and Mary have hired three sales people to work overlapping shifts, evenings and part time:

(a) April has previous experience in sales in a home accessory store.

(b) June is a university student whose previous experience has been with MacDonalds and as a camp counselor.

(c) Jim is a retired accountant.

After six months in business, John and Mary have concluded that while their advertising is attracting customers, the customers do not return after the initial visit. Sales have remained constant, but without repeat customers this could easily change. John and Mary decide they need to develop a customer relations program that will assure them a strong customer base. They are enthusiastic, willing to take part, and will accept criticism and new ideas.

Now, follow this case study as you read the remaining chapters of this book. You'll see how John and Mary were able to solve their problems and put an effective customer service program into place; and you'll see how the same ideas can work for you and your business.

3
THE VALUE OF SERVICE

Of the 12.6 million new jobs created in the United States since 1982, 85% were in the service industry. The growth in the number of two-income families has resulted in mass consumer services in travel, eating, and entertainment. New technology like computers, including training and software, has created services that were unheard of 20 years ago.

The result of these two changes in our society — the two-income family and more service-oriented businesses — is multiplied demands for service. Two-income families want convenience and quick, personal service. When they don't get it, the result is friction between frontline people and customers.

In large centers, anonymity can provide protection for those who give bad service: telephones can be hung up; it is impossible to argue with a recorded message; the copy machine mechanic is never the same person twice in a row. In small towns where you have a limited number of customers, buyer and seller know they will be meeting each other again and again. Service has a name and a face, and, more important, it has a reputation.

As we move into the twenty-first century, large service companies in large centers are beginning to recognize that service has a value, a dollar value, which is a conclusion the small service company in the small town recognized years ago when it hoisted the sign over the store that read "The Customer Is Number One" and always treated its clientele accordingly.

Measuring the value of good customer service may seem an impossible task. If you have a product to sell that is needed by a certain buying public, then, in theory, all you have to do is let the public know (advertise), sell it to them, and that is that. But it is not as simple as that. As we said earlier, people buy more than things; they buy expectations. They expect that what they buy will give them the benefits the seller or manufacturer promised and that it will work as promised. They also expect that if the product does not perform or produce as promised, the seller or manufacturer will make good on that promise.

If you are selling the same product as your competitor, the difference in success will be measured by how the customer is treated, both during and after the sale. Initially, you and your competitor start evenly matched. But it is the intangible cosseting and concern, the customer service, that adds value and makes the buyer return again and again. Then you have a very measurable assessment of service: the bottom line — the repeat customer — money — greater profits.

a. SETTING A VALUE ON YOUR SERVICE

Customer service is not a straight line that begins when the customer sees or hears your advertisement, takes a call from your salesperson and ends with the sale. It must continue long after the sale is made — until the next sale is made and then it must begin again.

Good customer service works in a circle, not a straight line. For example, suppose you are getting married and you seek out a photographer through an advertisement you have seen or on the recommendation of a friend. The photographer takes the pictures of your wedding. You like the pictures and buy those you want. For many photographers, that would be the end of the transaction. But a wise photographer, with a customer service program, will keep in touch with you letting you know when the studio is offering special events and sales. The photographer knows that, in time, you will want new pictures taken. You may start a family and want baby pictures. From there, you might want to commemorate anniversaries, birthdays, and graduations. It goes on from there, through the lifetime of your family and your family members. Good service creates a ripple effect. One circle can start another circle of new customers.

In setting a value on your customer service, you must first recognize that customers are self-centered. They really do not care about your problems. They care about their own problems and they want them solved. Customer loyalty, which translates into return buyers, comes from providing the products that solve problems and from providing service that satisfies customer expectation at all times. A good service plan has the system, both physical and procedural, that employees can use to meet their customers' expectations.

b. SETTING A VALUE ON CUSTOMER CONTACT

A customer relations program must first place a value on each contact the customer has with your people. The fewer contacts the customer has with your employees, the greater must be the quality of each contact. When a customer is buying a dress in a store, for example, the clerk is usually the only person she has contact with. If the clerk is rude, uninterested, or not cooperative, the customer judges the whole store by that one contact. The more contacts the customer has with personnel, the greater the opportunity for breakdown in customer service or, conversely, for repair of damaged customer service.

For example, when you go to the movies, you buy your ticket from the ticket seller, you give your ticket to the usher, and you buy your popcorn from someone else. If the ticket seller is rude, you may forget it if you are treated with special care by the usher and the popcorn seller. On the other hand, if the usher is also rude, you may not be placated by a gracious popcorn seller for you have already had two bad encounters. Wise business leaders recognize this kind of situation as three opportunities for good customer relations and emphasize the importance of service to every employee.

Every member of your organization must place a value on each opportunity they have to meet the customer or client. One dissatisfied customer will tell ten friends about the poor service or product. Those ten will tell ten more and soon your business reputation will snowball into an implacable negative value. Companies like Sony, IBM, General Electric and Whirlpool long ago recognized service as a marketing tool — part of the product sale. They place a high value on the service component. Maytag uses service as a major part of their advertising — the product is so good it leaves the Maytag repairman with nothing to do — but still the company is selling a service.

c. SERVICE AS A PRODUCT

If you find it difficult to place a value on service, think of it as a product:

(a) Service is produced at the instant of delivery. You can't keep boxes of it on the shelf. Like electricity you must produce it on demand.

(b) Service is delivered at the point of contact with the customer, by the frontline people, often beyond the control or influence of management or supervision.

(c) Service must be experienced by the customer at the moment it is delivered. It can't be sent out on approval.

(d) Service cannot be recalled, like a car for example. No one can bring it back for repairs. (You can offer apologies, but it's not the same. However, take heart; 95% of customers will buy again if a complaint is handled quickly and to their satisfaction.)

(e) Service is subjective. One person's idea of good service will differ from another's. You have to be prepared to deliver service to meet the varying standards: all sizes, all colors, in stock at all times!

d. THE VALUE OF EMPLOYEE PARTICIPATION

Remember that over 50% of customers rely on the opinions of their friends. Happy customers will be pleased to recommend you. The intangible service becomes tangible in the new customers you generate through your "product." Barkers Fine Dry Cleaning in Calgary has a way of measuring the value of a unique customer service which they look upon as a product. They provide coupons for one free dry cleaning to exclusive boutiques to give to their customers who buy an item from those particular boutiques. The follow-through that gives this service value is most important. When the customer brings the garment into Barkers to be cleaned for free, the customer treatment is first class. If they return to have their other clothing cleaned, Barkers have created a new, satisfied customer.

When a beauty parlor tried a similar scheme, it backfired. Young sales people handed out coupons door to door that gave the purchaser cut rates on beauty services. But the beauty parlor had not convinced their employees of the benefits of the plan. The employees, who were paid a commission on their work, received less money from the coupon holders and they were not convinced that the coupons might bring in more business in the long run. When the coupon customers made their appointments, they were greeted with derision. In several instances when callers mentioned the coupons while trying to make appointments, they were told that there were no openings with any operator so the cards became valueless. Bad publicity kept customers away instead of creating new ones.

Selling the value of service to employees must be your first consideration. In order to give service a value, the employees must be part of evaluating procedure. When taxi owners and drivers did this kind of evaluation, they realized that they had a poor reputation for customer service, so they developed their "Miami Nice" customer relations training program for taxi drivers. The rewards of the program were so great that it became U.S.A. Nice and is now being used in Canada as well.

When you and your employees place a high value on service, the result is profit. In order to offer service that has value, you and your employees must consider service to be a product. That product is "sold" every time an employee has contact with a customer. Enthusiastic, cooperative personnel who know the value of service and who work together in harmony attract customers. Instead of having the company go to the market, the market comes to the company, and the company becomes more profitable.

e. EVALUATING YOUR SERVICE

You, your supervisors, and your managers need to ask the following questions and come to a consensus on the answers.

(a) How many employees do my clients or customers come in contact with before the sale is completed?

(b) How many employees do clients or customers come in contact with after the sale is completed? (Delivery, service, etc.)

(c) If one of those people stopped the sale from being completed, what minimum value, in dollars, could the company lose? (Your lowest product price.)

(d) If one of those people stopped the sale from happening, what maximum value, in dollars, could the company lose? (Your highest product price.)

(e) What would be the average loss of a sale? (Total of the minimum plus the maximum divided by two.)

(f) Based on the average loss of a sale, if the disgruntled customer told ten other people (potential clients) what would be the total loss of the sale? (Multiply the average cost by 11; i.e., the loss of the sale to the initial customer plus the potential loss of 10 customers.)

(g) Divide that total loss (answer to (f)) by the number of employees a customer contacts before, during, and after the sale. You now have the value of each customer contact. True, it is hypothetical, but it gives you an idea of the dollar value that good service can bring to your company.

CASE STUDY

When John and Mary evaluated the service at The ABC Shoppe, they found that the customer usually came into contact with just one employee, right at the point of sale, with no follow-up contact for delivery or service. The lowest priced item in their store was a pair of small scissors that could be carried in a pocket or purse ($5.95). The highest priced item was a silk blouse ($398.00). Therefore, the average loss of sale would be $201.98. The total loss of one dissatisfied customer could mean a potential loss of $2,221.78 ($201.98 x 11 lost customers). Seen in those terms, John and Mary realized the value of good customer service; it meant the difference between paying the rent or not!

4
DEVELOPING A PROFITABLE CUSTOMER RELATIONS PROGRAM

Any plan for improvement needs people. You can lavish care on trend lines, graphs, pie charts, and diagrams and lovingly produce blueprints that are works of art, but, eventually, somebody, somewhere, somehow has to transform those good intentions into reality. That is when you must depend on your employees.

It takes human energy and ingenuity to turn the potential into practice, to make the promise come alive, to lift fragile words off paper and turn them into a dynamic human force. Woe betide the company that thinks the hard part is over when the plans are approved. The task has just begun.

Many companies, enamored of their plans, pay homage to the piles of paper, while ignoring the human aspect of the process. They just assume people will understand. Even more perilous is the assumption that people will automatically agree with the proposals. The result is their energetic program evolves into a static display in the basement vault, and once in a while the senior people must muse on what might have been if only the "others" had cooperated.

So let's put the horse back in front of the cart and start with your most important resource: your people.

a. DEVELOPING EMPLOYEE SUPPORT

1. Getting their attention

Wise organizations know cooperation is the keystone for progress. They realize and acknowledge that their employees are the vehicle by which the organization can prosper and grow. But to do so the employees must also prosper and grow, so it makes sense for management to invest in the development of its people by enlarging their knowledge base and including them in the planning process.

It's a two-way street. As employees' confidence and skills improve so do their contributions to the company because they have a keener interest in their careers. It's a mushrooming process. The more they feel they are contributing the more they feel a part of the total company family; they are investing a portion of themselves in the organization.

Have you ever heard a person proudly talk about "my company"? There is the often told story of Marshall Field, owner of the giant Field's Department store chain in Chicago who was walking through the various departments of the store and overheard an employee's little girl talking to another about "my daddy's" store and "my daddy's" customers. The child's mother recognized Mr. Field and started to apologize for her daughter's chatter about the store belonging to her daddy. Mr. Field interrupted her by saying, "If only I could get more employees to think of the store as their own."

Despite what most pessimists say, the proprietary glow still burns in the hearts of many employees. It's a precious resource, and you can rekindle that flame, then fan it into a bright and glowing attitude, by letting employees know they are important.

But first you need to get their attention. Old style management would have suggested that a two-by-four across the back of the neck was a good way to get attention. Maybe it would work for a while, but the attention would be fleeting, at most, and soon pushed out of mind by resentment of the crude way it was handled.

Today we have more effective ways to get people's attention. In 1979, Studs Terkel, author of the best selling book

Working, spoke in San Francisco at the annual convention of the International Association of Business Communicators. He talked about how he had interviewed workers all across the United States. In one instance he ate lunch with a steelworker, perched high on the steel framework of a burgeoning new skyscraper. When questioned about the major component missing from his job, the steelworker said it was recognition. "When the building is completed," he said, "nobody will ever know I worked on it. I can't even bring my children to show them my handiwork because it will be all encased in concrete."

Questioned further, the steelworker came up with an idea to counter the lack of recognition. He suggested that a stainless steel strip with the name of every contributor engraved on it be fastened to the side of the building where it could be easily seen.

When you think about it, we're not talking about business logic, but emotion, one of the most powerful forces we can harness. People make decisions based on emotion, then justify them afterward with logic. First you need to win your employees' hearts, then you'll be able to capture their minds.

So, to firmly grasp the interest of your people, and then maintain it, you need to give them recognition. You need a steel strip firmly fixed in everybody's mind that tells them over and again that they are important and they are recognized.

2. Getting them motivated

It has been said that you cannot motivate other people...they have to motivate themselves. This may be so, but you can certainly provide the ammunition for your employees or coworkers to motivate themselves. It is part of a manager's role to show people how to get excited, enthused, and energetic about their new and expanded responsibilities; and we do mean show them, not tell them. Yet few managers know where to begin.

The pivotal word is belonging. A sense of belonging is crucial as a motivating factor. When people feel they are contributing their personal talents to a worthwhile endeavor, then they have a stake in that enterprise. They adopt a personal responsibility, become committed, and, best of all, start developing pride — pride in themselves and pride in the work they perform. To get people motivated you have to put them back in the picture, convince them that their contribution is valuable, give them responsibility, and allow them to use their creativity.

In the past, our society has stifled much creative thought. Many areas have been taken over by robots and the responsibility of decision-making has been removed. Creativity and thinking by employees was viewed almost as subversive. How many times have you heard a manager or employer say, "Why would they want to think anyway? We do it for them. They just have to show up and do what they're told."

Yet machines still cannot think, they cannot reason, nor can they make subjective judgment calls or decisions that require emotional considerations. Finally we have acknowledged these facts and the feudal attitude in business and industry is yielding to a growing awareness that the real resource of any organization is its people. They are no longer pawns but important centers of influence. Properly motivated they can be the difference between success or failure, between profit or loss.

3. Getting them involved

Get your employees involved at the outset in helping to define and then develop your plan. Ask them for ideas. Have them on the task force or the steering committee, whatever you call it, but get them involved.

Most people would agree that commitment is paramount to any sustained program of customer relations, but commitment is not achieved on a casual basis. There has to be a reason for people to commit themselves to an ideal or a cause. They can't commit themselves wholeheartedly unless they know what it is they are committing themselves to and why. In other words, they must understand the reason why you are asking for their assistance.

If they can develop an understanding of the plan and their role in it, then involvement can be the next step. Get them involved in the early stages of planning.

Here's a note of warning. People will only be as effective as the leaders they follow. They will not commit themselves further or involve themselves more deeply than their immediate managers do. So if you have managers who are only paying lip service to newly developed plans, lip service will be the order of the day for all their subordinates.

4. Getting them encouraged

Encouragement is another powerful business tool, and yet sadly it's the one most overlooked. It's not neglected deliberately; in fact, most people recognize what a potent force it can be, but it is easy to say, "Well, we don't have the time or the inclination right now. Besides, next year looks much brighter...with more potential."

Let's state it frankly. Without encouragement people become robots, performing acceptable tasks at barely acceptable levels. Why? They have no invested interest in their work, and by implication the organization has no invested interest in them. Yet time and again we hear managers complain that loyalty seems to have evaporated along with the ethic of "an hour's pay for an hour's work."

Ask yourself if loyalty has really gone the way of the dodo bird and silently slipped away, or has it been stifled, crushed, and ignored in the blind pursuit of profit and the rush for clinical efficiency? In a solid-state world we sometimes forget we're dealing with fluid-state people.

Academic theories aside, if loyalty has disappeared or died, can it be restored or revitalized? It has been done before, but it has taken time, and, above all, commitment — long-term commitment. Why not avoid the pain of restoration. Start off on the right foot. Begin with encouragement — given sincerely and at appropriate times.

b. PUTTING IT TOGETHER

We've talked about the steps necessary to get employees interested in a customer service plan. They include getting the employees' attention, getting them motivated, getting them involved, and then getting them encouraged. The question is how to tie all this together so it makes sense, and makes them want to be a part of the program.

Tell them what's in it for them! Talk about benefits, the rewards, the prestige they will gain by becoming active in this program. As you talk about the benefits, emphasize the personal aspects of involvement, how they can personally grow by playing an active role as an individual or on the team, and about becoming committed.

Then, to ensure they remain committed once they are involved in the planning process, help them view the customer relations program as theirs. If they can recognize themselves or their contribution in some aspect of the plan, then it will become "their" plan. Design a recognition program by answering how employees will be rewarded for —

(a) Providing input to the formulation of the program (i.e., serving on a planning committee or task force)

(b) Implementing the program

(c) Maintaining the program (You will want to review this after three months, six months, and one year)

(d) Increasing revenue through the customer relations program

(e) Creating a stronger public image (e.g., involvement in the community outside of business that reflects positively on the business)

(f) Augmenting the program with new ideas, new methods, new procedures ("Suggestion box" contributions that are used should be rewarded. Continued committee work for monitoring and assessment should be rewarded.)

Recognition can be provided by verbal praise, monetary gifts, plaques, etc. Rewards should be given before peers to fully recognize the contribution of the employee and to provide an incentive for other employees.

You may decide that an annual meeting is most appropriate where major achievements can be publicly recognized. Alternatively, you may decide on a less formal semi-annual meeting in addition to the larger meeting to increase the interest at the local level. Stories and feature articles in the organization's newsletter are an ideal and economical way to show appreciation. Small dinner parties and special events are also good ways to focus attention on your commitment to the program.

We said earlier that good communication is a journey, not a destination. The same applies to encouragement and the benefit is that it pays off — big.

When you include your people from the outset, the bonus is you will receive advice from the frontline troops, the people in the trenches who look eyeball to eyeball with your customers on a daily basis. They are the experts. Why not tap that knowledge? It's a compliment to your employees that you want to listen to them and their advice. But it's also a big boost to their self-esteem when you acknowledge their expertise by including their suggestions in your customer service plan. When a person's self-esteem rises, so does the morale in that particular office, or area. It rubs off on others because as humans we don't want to be left out...we don't want to miss anything.

c. A SIMPLE PLAN THAT WORKS

Most simple plans work. It is when we get fancy and add frills, or when we plan to impress, rather than express, that we run into trouble. So, assuming you have your employees onside, that they want to become involved, and that they are anxious to get rolling, then here is a simple formula that works. You can add to it, enlarge it, reduce it, change it or adapt it, depending on what you and your people decide; but it will help you get started, and you can start right away.

Most problem solving starts with research; we have chosen the RACE formula to help you get yourself launched. RACE stands for Research, Action, Communication, and Evaluation.

To follow the formula, you need to work through a series of steps. It may take some time because the value of a program developed depends on how well the goals are defined. The clearer the goals, the better they can be understood, and when they are understood and properly acted upon, then they are measured, and measurement is how you determine how successful your program is in meeting customer needs and in meeting your objectives.

(a) Know intimately the policies, goals, and objectives of your organization.

(b) Analyze your various customers/clients/employees and their significance to you.

(c) Assess your reputation with each of your customers/clients/employees, and the potential for improvement.

(d) Decide what actions are required and the strategy to achieve them.

(e) Plan your program.

(f) Implement the program.

(g) Monitor its progress and results.

(h) Revise and adjust where necessary.

If you follow through on the eight steps above, you will find out why people respond to you and your business in a particular manner and how you can design your responses to get them on your side rather than in opposition.

Let's go through each of the eight areas in more detail.

(a) Knowing your organization may sound redundant, but ask 20 employees coming out of an office at 5:30 p.m. why they are in business and you will get some interesting replies. If you know your organization thoroughly, then you can plan for its growth. You can talk about it sensibly and confidently and with conviction. And, frankly, you better know more about your business than your competitors because they will be exploiting your weaknesses before you know that those weaknesses exist. Above all, don't forget to communicate your thoughts and ideas. (See chapter 7.)

(b) Once you have a solid grasp on who you are, what you do, and why, then you can turn your attention to knowing your customers/clients/employees. You can analyze them, examine the problems, differences, and barriers between them and you, and then determine the potential for improvement. And let's face it, is there a single organization in North America that couldn't stand having its image polished? Remember to communicate your findings.

(c) Assess your reputation with each of your customers/clients/employees. See if you can discover the reason for your reputation, good or bad. Is it justified, can it be changed, are there any benefits if it is changed? What is your image now? What would you like it to be? What do people really think of your organization? Communicate your results or findings.

(d) Decide what actions are required and the strategy needed to ensure the success of your program. What do you want your reputation to be? What do you want people to think of you and your organization? Communicate your strategy to employees.

(e) Plan your program. Use input and advice from all employees to uncover your customers' wants and needs, their likes and dislikes, their incomes, attitudes preferences, or biases. The more you know about them, the more your plans can reflect their lifestyles. Your aim should be to get both employees and customers thinking in terms of "my business." Remember, communicate your plans.

(f) The implementation of your plan should receive the same care and attention as the planning process. How and when you put the plan into effect can affect the overall success of your venture. It has to be done logically, deliberately, step-by-step, anchoring one segment firmly in place before moving on to the next. If there are delays, tell people and tell them why. If changes are needed, keep them informed. Better still, ask for help. Continually communicate the process.

(g) Monitoring a customer service program requires fortitude. It requires "stick-to-it-iveness," persistence, a hang in there attitude to overcome the tendency to settle back in your chair. When so much energy has been poured into the previous steps of planning the process, the urge is to launch it and leave it...if the darn thing floats then you have been successful. Unfortunately this is the point where many finely crafted programs flounder; much the same as launching a luxury liner, initially it's the keel that slides down, with much work still to be done inside and up top. When you launch your program you will find much work still to be done: fine-tuning, polishing and plugging leaks. And as with an ocean-going ship, maintenance is ongoing. Communicate progress.

(h) Revising a plan can be difficult, but if it needs to be done, then do it quickly. Once again, get input and solutions from your employees. You don't do anyone a favor by waffling when you should be deciding. If changes are necessary, act promptly. Let employees know about the changes and the reasons they were adopted. When you keep people informed they are more sympathetic to the cause and to the frustration you encounter. Often they will be moved enough to put forward alternative suggestions, particularly if they view their actions as one team member coming to the aid of another. Again, communicate changes, and the reasons for them.

d. DO-IT-YOURSELF FLOWCHART

The figure on the page 33 is a flowchart to help you get your plan started. Pick the topics and areas you feel most appropriate to your situation, but do it now. Chart out roughly your ideas, and then read on for ideas on setting goals and implementing your ideas.

CASE STUDY

John and Mary decided it was time to involve the employees of The ABC Shoppe. A meeting seemed a good way to start to review the store's performance and listen to employees' concerns too. To help understand the store's objectives, John prepared some simple charts.

They held a staff meeting at a time that was agreeable to all. The staff was paid for attending the meeting. John reviewed the six months they had been in business and he pointed out that while revenues were constant, they signified no growth and it was obvious that there was a lack of customer return and loyalty.

Mary reported the results on their evaluation of service (see chapter 3), and John introduced the idea of a customer service program and how to go about preparing one for the store. Using a flow chart he designed himself, John discussed each step. Both he and Mary encouraged all the staff to take part in the discussion.

While everybody agreed there was a need for improved customer relations, it was immediately apparent there was also a need to set some goals for the program. They did that by following the advice in the next chapter.

FIGURE #1
DO-IT-YOURSELF FLOWCHART

START BY RESEARCHING THESE AREAS

Business organization
Management objectives & organization
Suppliers and creditors
Business policies
The products or services we supply
Community
Employees (and labor unions)
Stockholders
Customer/client relations, including areas
Competitorsof interests
Marketing program
Customers

**THEN ANALYZE WHAT YOU HAVE DISCOVERED
IN TERMS OF**

Business objectives
Customer service problems and interests
Capabilities — the company's, the staff's
Growth factors

**WHEN YOU KNOW YOUR STRENGTHS
AND WEAKNESSES, THEN DESIGN YOUR
STRATEGY TO ACHIEVE**

Business objectives
Marketing objectives

PLAN THE PROGRAM TO GET RESULTS

Objectives
Customers/clients to be reached
Implementing the program
Methods to be used
Results expected

IMPLEMENT THE PLAN
People
Place
Time

MONITOR AND ADJUST
Check
Review
Advise

5
SETTING GOALS FOR YOUR BUSINESS

When business people are honest, they say they are in business to make money, and there is nothing wrong with that. But the manner in which you make that money can be affected by the image and reputation the company wishes to create. If you are in business to make money in a very short time, image and reputation may not be a high priority. But if you plan to be around for any length of time, then they become very important. Before you can have a successful customer relations program, you must make some very important decisions about image and reputation, quality and performance. The Japanese have shown us that putting quality first did not increase costs, but actually increased profits. The Disney corporation sets very high standards for the image, reputation, and quality of its operations of Disneyland and Disney World. The result has been world wide esteem and a very healthy business.

a. WHY ARE YOU IN BUSINESS?

Answer these questions, honestly. No one is looking over your shoulder.

  (a) Am I in business to make a profit?

  (b) Am I in business for the long haul?

  (c) Is my personal reputation important to me?

  (d) Is my company's reputation important to me?

  (e) Is customer satisfaction important to the success of my business?

(f) Is the repeat customer important to my business?

(g) Do I plan to be in this particular town or city for a period of time?

(h) If my business expanded, would my reputation and my company's reputation in this area still be important to me?

John and Mary of our case study answered all these questions with a strong "yes." If *you* answered yes to the above questions, then image and reputation are important to you and your business. But you need to define clearly what you want that image and reputation to be. This should be the first step in the research for your customer service program. Ask yourself the following questions, then have your employees answer the same questions, individually.

(a) Describe what this business is in business for.

(b) Why would you recommend people do business with this organization?

(c) Why do you work for this company?

(d) What is the greatest satisfaction you get from working for this company?

Compare your responses to those of your employees. Is there a correlation of perception or a marked difference? Employees who have a genuine interest and pride in their work and the company project that pride, and it is this same pride that builds a company's positive reputation.

CASE STUDY

When John and Mary compared their answers to those of their employees, they found some differences. While June's answers were more like their own and showed a strong leaning toward the customer, recognition of good service, and the satisfaction of doing a job well, Jim's perception was solely to make money for himself and the business. April's replies showed a strong concentration on the satisfaction gained from keeping order. The customer and customer satisfaction were not included in any of her replies.

b. WHAT ARE YOUR PRODUCTS AND SERVICES?

You can't be in business unless you have a product or service to sell, but have you clearly defined what they are for yourself and your employees? If you are in the restaurant business, you are obviously selling food, but what else are you selling? Relaxation? Comfort? Self-esteem? Pampering? Quick service? Eye appeal? Tried and true fare or something new and adventurous? Each restaurant is selling food, but each one is also selling other services, depending on the vision of the owners and employees as well as the expectations of the customers.

Ask yourself these questions:

(a) What is your principle product or service?

(b) What other tangible products or services are you selling?

(c) What intangible products or services are you selling?

- Ambiance?
- Pride?
- Self-esteem?
- Reliability?
- Dependability?

Make your own list.

You have probably noticed that many commercials and advertisements do not discuss the product, instead they project the image of how you will feel about yourself when driving this particular car, using that particular computer, washing your hair with this shampoo — all intangibles but part of the product or service.

CASE STUDY

When John and Mary asked themselves these questions, they found that while they took pride in the quality of their merchandise, their discussion brought up other considerations — some intangibles that they had overlooked. As a quality boutique they were not selling just shirts or accessories, they were selling pride — pride in looking and dressing well. They were also selling reliability: "You can count on us to always bring you unique, quality merchandise." They were also selling dependability: "You can depend on us to provide you with the products you want and we will stand behind anything we sell."

c. WHO ARE YOUR CUSTOMERS OR CLIENTS?

You may have the best product or service in the world, but the sale is not made until the customer pays for it. Before you went into business, you should have researched your client base so you would know whom to approach to make that sale. It has often been said that when you open a business there are three very important things to consider: location, location, location. But now that you are properly located and in business, you know that there is more to it than that. You need to know everything possible about your customers. Sports teams have taken this concept further than anybody; they review videotapes of their opponents' plays and players, then design strategy (game plan) to improve their chances of winning.

To design your game plan and maximize your opportunities for winning, ask yourself and your employees these questions:

(a) Who should be buying your products/services?

(b) Why should they buy your products/services?

(c) Who is buying your products/services?

(d) Why are they buying?

(e) Are you well located to serve your customers?

(f) Are you open the hours to give them service?

(g) What else should you be offering your customers but are not?

(h) Why aren't you offering it, or at least thinking about it?

From the answers to these questions, you can determine if you and your employees agree about the public you should be serving. If you disagree, you need to resolve your customer definition. You may also want to explore the possibilities of attracting a new customer base.

CASE STUDY

When the owners and employees of The ABC Shoppe answered these questions, they found they could easily answer the first six. They were aiming for and getting a clientele of middle and upper income customers who bought quality, fine-crafted, unique items for themselves or as gifts. The problem came in answering the last two questions. They came to the conclusion that even though their merchandise was good, the location was excellent, and they stayed open at the proper times, they were treating their customers poorly or without courtesy.

When they thought about what they should be offering their customers, but were not, they concluded that they needed to give their customers personal attention and courteous, polite service. They should be demonstrating concern about satisfying the customers, and they should be warm and enthusiastic about their merchandise. After all, if they aren't excited about it, why should the customer be excited? They also decided that they should be developing a friendly, non-threatening climate that invites people to return.

The answer to the last question was simple, but nobody had taken the time to think about it. The business was new and everybody was so wrapped up in their own responsibilities that unplanned events like brain storming or creative thinking were pushed on the back burner. Everyone had the attitude "Why think about the store in my own free time?"

d. WHAT DO YOUR CUSTOMERS AND CLIENTS EXPECT?

We keep repeating that a customer relations program is built on expectations, but do you really know what your customers or clients expect from doing business with you? Part of your research should determine those expectations. If you have a steady client base, you can easily mail out a postage-paid reply card asking questions such as the following:

(a) What do you like about our product (or service, store, restaurant, etc.)?

(b) What would you change about our product (or service, etc.)?

(c) Has our customer service been to your satisfaction?

(d) What improvements would you like to see, items changed or added? How can we improve?

(e) Have our employees treated you with respect and courtesy?

(f) How can they be of greater service?

(g) What else can we do to make your work (visit, dining, etc.) easier (better) for you?

Hotels and restaurants often ask customers to fill out a card or the back of the bill regarding service. If you employ this method as a means to gain consumer reaction, be sure to follow through and act upon the comments. Just recently we spent considerable time filling in such a restaurant service enquiry, itemizing the details we thought were important. We filled in the place asking for our telephone number, but we still haven't heard from the restaurant.

If a customer stops doing business with you, you need to find out why. While some dissatisfied people are very vocal, others are not. A non-threatening phone call can get to the heart of the matter. In your research, you should go back over your client list and determine why a customer may have stopped doing business with you.

CASE STUDY

When John and Mary used a reply card to get a sampling of customer reaction, they found customers liked the merchandise and the store itself, but found the service inconsistent. One reply gave details of being rebuked by April, "We would never promise you that." Another pointed out that Jim seemed in a hurry to get the sale over with. A number of replies commented on June's good nature and obvious interest in them, but pointed out that the way she was dressed did not reflect the image of the store. One rather proper respondent added that June's use of slang such as "yeah," "you know," and "okay" detracted from her other good qualities. It was pointed out that there was no gift wrapping provided, yet many customers were buying gifts so this would be a convenient service. Finally, customers noted that when they asked if they could be telephoned when a certain item came in, they were told that the procedure "wasn't store policy."

Ask similar questions of yourself and your staff:

(a) What do you think our customers like about our product (service, store, restaurant, etc.)?

(b) What do you think they would change about our product (service, etc.)?

(c) Do you think our customer service has been to our customers' satisfaction?

(d) If not, what do you think they would want changed about our service?

(e) Do you think we treat our customers with respect and courtesy?

(f) How could we be of greater service to our customers?

(g) What could we do to make our customers work (visit, dining, etc.) easier, better for them?

(h) Are the telephones being answered politely?

(i) How often and for how long are customers kept on hold?

(j) How many calls are being transferred? How many are lost in transfer?

(k) How many complaints do we receive by telephone daily, weekly, and monthly? What categories do the complaints fall into?

(l) How are complaints by telephone being handled? Who is responsible for handling complaints?

(m) When complaints are resolved, how is this monitored? What is the follow-up to the complaint?

(n) Are any complaints left unresolved?

Once you have discovered your customers' expectations of your products and services, you will need to compare them with yours and those of your employees, to see how closely they relate. From the information gathered, you can determine —

(a) Status quo

(b) Changes needed

(c) How to make the changes

(d) How to put the changes into perspective

(e) How to monitor new practices

(f) How to assess results

(g) How to make adjustments

(h) How to introduce adjustments

(i) How to evaluate adjustments

(j) How to communicate steps to personnel

(k) What training is needed

You can design other questionnaires for other customer contact situations. You may be very surprised at some of the client answers to your questions. We can tell you that cleanliness ranks next to godliness with some customers. That's cleanliness of the physical plant, office or store, the employees, even the person who makes the deliveries. Make sure that your customer expectations of your company are not being corroded by a subliminal image. Untidy files, unwashed windows, shoes behind doors, out-of-date posters and general untidiness can make a strong impression on people. An agricultural firm did a survey of their clients and found that the general appearance of their building was having a very negative effect. One reply stated, "How can you be in the business of working with farmers when you have such a healthy growth of pig weed and Russian thistle bordering your property? No self-respecting farmer would tolerate those weeds choking out the grass."

CASE STUDY

When John and Mary looked at the replies from their staff and themselves, they found that Jim believed they were giving the customers good service and could not think of any changes to make. April agreed with him. June felt none of the staff was friendly enough. She also felt that the staff members were sometimes too concerned with the work they were doing (e.g., stocking shelves) and did not give the customer the attention they should. She also brought up the fact that April often corrected her in front of customers or broke in on what she was saying to a customer. John and Mary didn't think their customers were getting the kind of service they expected and often demanded themselves when they shopped, but they found it difficult to change roles to become service oriented.

e. WHO IS YOUR COMPETITION?

There are hundreds of restaurants in every city. Have you ever wondered why one stays in business for years while scores of others disappear within months? There are now a multitude of computer outlets offering both hardware and software products. Why do those identical products have successes and failures? In many cases, it is because new business owners haven't researched their competition. Never run down a competitor to a customer or client, but be aware of what they are doing right and wrong. Keeping ahead of the competition means learning from their successes and failures. Ask yourself these questions:

   (a) How long have they been in business?

   (b) What is their reputation for product/service?

   (c) What are they doing that we don't do?

   (d) Is it attracting more customers/clients for them?

   (e) If we are both doing the same thing, how can we do it better?

CASE STUDY

The competition for The ABC Shoppe came from a well-established specialty store eight blocks away. It did not have as great a variety of merchandise and it was not as attractive. However, it did have a regular and steady clientele. The third question — What are they doing that we don't do? — was the important one for John and Mary. They found their competitor's sales staff accommodating and friendly with a focus on serving the customer, even phoning a competitive store to find an item if necessary. The store also had a mailing list for special promotions and a customer-pay gift wrapping service.

f. HOW DO YOU RATE RIGHT NOW?

Conduct a customer relations internal/external audit as part of your research.

(a) Are telephones being answered courteously? Is the information that is being given correct? Is the tone of voice warm and friendly? Can you understand the name of the company or is it being "sung" or said so quickly it can't be understood?

(b) Are customers approached with vitality, interest, and enthusiasm, but without aggressive behavior?

(c) Are customers being allowed privacy to make decisions, explore possibilities, and confer with companions?

(d) Are customer complaints and inquiries received in a respectful, agreeable manner and acted upon promptly and efficiently?

(e) Is correspondence answered promptly and in the proper tone?

(f) Are messages taken and handled efficiently and graciously?

(g) Are business facilities well maintained?

(h) Does the staff pay attention to good grooming, decorum, and personal image? Does their personal image reflect the image of the company?

(i) Do staff provide the extra time and attention to make a customer feel special and important to the business?

(j)   Are products checked before delivery to make sure they are in proper working order and as specified by the buyer?

(k)   Does the product arrive on time and in proper working condition?

(l)   Is there follow-up to ensure the customer is satisfied?

(m) Is there follow-up to make sure the customer returns?

(n)   Are personnel being told they have done a good job?

Several years ago, we had the opportunity to ride in the taxi cab of a man who had obviously asked himself all these questions. The cab was on older model Rolls Royce, immaculate inside and out. The driver-owner was equally well groomed. When we got into the cab, and, yes, he held the door for you, we found the tiny vases filled with fresh flowers. Before the cab started we were asked our destination, which of the three daily papers we wanted to read, whether we would prefer a tape of classical, pop, or western music, silence, or the radio station of our choice. The only other question was whether we had visited the city before. When we said we had, but only on business, we were asked if we had time to take a little swing around some of the more interesting areas. Suspecting that we would be facing a much larger fee than the straight ride to the hotel, we hesitated. He assured us that there would be no extra charge and true to his word he shut off the meter and took us on a little excursion through some of the more interesting parts of Toronto. Needless to say, he received a generous tip and was referred to all our associates. Here was a man who loved his work, had respect for his clients, was interested in their welfare, and worked hard to meet their expectations. But he also worked hard to meet his own expectations and even though he had been singled out by customers and journalists for the quality of his business, he never bought another cab or hired anyone to work for him. He said he wanted to remain small and in complete control. He set high expectations for himself, and his reputation confirmed that quality of service was important to him and, ultimately, to his customers.

CASE STUDY

By performing an audit as discussed above, John and Mary found that there was inconsistency in how the telephone was answered depending on who did the answering. June best conveyed the tone and image they wished, except she used slang. Jim was businesslike, but almost too brisk, and April was sometimes almost hostile.

John and Mary found the three employees were not greeting the customers or offering discreet assistance. They were leaving the customers too much on their own. The maintenance of the store was also inconsistent. Sometimes it opened on time, sometimes it did not. Sometimes the counters were cleaned and tidied, sometimes not. April and Jim were the most consistent in these areas.

There was no follow-through to assure customer satisfaction or to ensure that a customer returned.

Finally, the audit showed that the employees received no monetary or other tangible rewards and verbal praise was sporadic at best.

g. SETTING GOALS

From the information you have gathered, you can confidently set goals for your business. To do so, carefully go though each of the following steps.

(a) Determine why you are in business. Ask not only yourself, but your employees. Do you have the same perceptions? If they differ, why?

(b) Identify clearly what you are offering your clients. Products? Services? (Both the tangible and the intangible.) Once again this a project for both you and your employees. What are the differences between your perceptions and theirs?

(c) Determine who your clients are. Do you and your employees agree? Can you enlarge the client base?

(d) Determine what your clients expect from your products/services.

(e) Determine your competition. Identify their successful and unsuccessful customer/client relations strategies.

(f) Conduct a customer/client relations audit of your company's operating procedures.

(g) Determine the goals for your business or company.

(h) Once your goals have been set then you can determine the action to achieve the goal.

Use the worksheet on page 49 to work out your own goals for your customer relations program.

CASE STUDY

As a result of the surveys done by the customers, the employees and owners of The ABC Shoppe, John set up two task forces to establish goals for the store. The first task force consisted of June and Mary. Their task was to determine ways to better service customers, to attract new customers, and to assure repeated patronage.

John felt that June had the customer's concerns at heart and that Mary had the "shopper's point of view." Mary also had a traveler's knowledge of what other, similar stores were doing.

The second task force consisted of Jim and April. Their task was to evaluate present staff skills, determine training needed, and suggest rewards for a job well done.

By giving Jim and April the staffing goals, John felt he could involve them in an area where both needed help. At the same time, they could capitalize on their obvious skills for creating order and giving attention to detail.

John was not without a task. He set himself up as a committee of one to assure consistency in the day-to-day operation of the store.

The task forces were given paid time to meet and a date was set for reporting to a staff meeting.

In the next chapter, you will see the format the employees at The ABC Shoppe decided was best for them.

1. Why are we in business?

My perception	Employee's perceptions	Differences	Why differences?	Goal

2. Services, products (both tangible and intangible)

My perception	Employee's perceptions	Differences	Why differences?	Goal

3. Our customers

My perception	Employee's perceptions	Differences	Why differences?	Goal

4. Customer/Client expectations (research)

My perception	Employee's perceptions	Differences	Why differences?	Goal

SETTING GOALS — Continued

5. Competition
Who are they?

What are they doing well?	What mistakes are they making?	What can we do better than them?	Goal

6. Customer /Client relations audit
What are we doing well?

What are we doing badly?	What can we change?	What shouldn't we change?	Goal

---

Goals can be set to —

1. Make employer-employee perceptions the same, achieve a compromise or a new perception.
2. Make customer-employer-employee perceptions the same, achieve a compromise or a new perception.
3. Adapt other business strategies that will improve basic customer relations.
4. Assure that the status of present procedures does not change.
5. Make present procedures better.
6. Introduce new procedures that will assure better customer service.

6
PUTTING YOUR PLAN TOGETHER

a. PLANNING YOUR SUCCESS

The old adage "when we fail to plan, we plan to fail" is particularly relevant to customer service. Whether through procrastination, laziness, ignorance, or indifference, if we ignore the planning process today, we are laying the foundation for failure tomorrow.

Let's assume that ignorance is the major culprit, and the majority of us are unfamiliar with planning — particularly a new venture. The first questions that surface are "Where do I begin?" and "What are the precedents to guide me?" It's this stage of planning, taking the first wobbly steps, that can be most daunting.

We could contemplate it more, but like other business people, the more we dwell on the problem, the larger it looms, and any problem can quickly assume mammoth proportions, even creating second thoughts about the wisdom of venturing into unfamiliar territory.

b. BITE-SIZED CHUNKS: DEVELOPING TASK FORCES

The solution is to cut it down to size, preferably into chunks, that can be understood, accepted, and assimilated. Much like golf, no seasoned player would expect a hole-in-one on a 400-yard fairway. Instead, he or she would plan a series of approach shots, using different clubs to suit the terrain and the distance the ball is required to travel. Using this system, the golfer concentrates on the immediate shot, using the driver or iron most appropriate for the approach rather than filling the mind with fanciful images of the putter when the green is the size of a dime on the horizon. "First things first," sums it up aptly.

Developing a plan for customer relations has to be done logically and in an orderly manner, and yet, like golf, it can be frustrating, unpredictable, and sometimes wearying. But the elation that comes from a winning strategy and consistently better performance makes it all worthwhile.

Setting up task forces can be a useful means to organize the various facets of your plan. If you decide to use this method, follow these steps to guide your task forces:

(a) Determine the need for a task force

- Do you want input from all personnel?

- Do you want a consensus of opinion?

- Do you want commitment to the proposal of a customer relations program?

If you answer yes to these questions, then establish a task force.

(b) Determine the objective for a task force

- What do you want it to accomplish?

- Do not give it too many topics or too broad a mandate to cover. You may need more than one task force.

(c) Determine the responsibilities of the task force

- What is the agenda for the task force?

- What is expected of the task force? For example, if the task force is to determine the customers' perception of the company, will it devise methods of research, implement the research, evaluate the research, support the status quo, or bring about change?

(d) Determine reporting strategy

- At what point(s) in its agenda does the task force report back to the planning committee? Set a time frame for interim and final reporting.

(e) Determine the makeup and numbers of the task force

- Ensure that there is representation from all areas immediately concerned by the agenda.

- Ensure there is representation from all areas affected by the agenda over a period of time.

- Keep to workable numbers to allow for maximum discussion.

(f) Select a chair for the task force

- A chair can be selected by the committee itself or by appointment or volunteers and can be anyone from the loading dock to the front desk. (For more information on meeting formats and guidelines, see *The Business Guide to Effective Speaking*, another title in the Self-Counsel Business Series.)

(g) Develop a work plan for the task force

- A work plan can be developed by the task force itself or by working in conjunction with a program development leader.

- Identify objective of task force.

- Identify steps to reach objective.

- Put steps in order of importance.

- Establish a time frame for reaching the objective.

- Establish a time frame for completing each step.

- Allocate responsibilities.

- Establish a regular schedule of routine meetings.

- Gain commitment from all concerned.

c. A FOUNDATION FOR PLANNING

In chapter 4, we used a flow chart to show how to develop a program for your organization. One section of that flow chart was on planning the program, which covered five major areas.

In planning your program, you may decide you need more than five areas or you may discover you can combine some areas under one heading. There is no hard and fast rule. The criterion is whatever is best for your organization at this time.

d. THE EASY STEP-BY-STEP PLAN

Obviously the first draft will not be a perfect plan, nor will it be the most comprehensive, but it will get you started on the planning activity. In the process, you will overcome the mental block that often arises when you face something for the first time.

So let's work through the planning process together. Go through the following questions and note your answers on a piece of paper. As you work your way down the page, you will see signposts emerge — conclusions that will point you in the right direction, letting you know what is needed, what would be nice to have, and what you should discard.

Because this type of planning process may be new to you, we want to be sure to capture your undivided attention for about 10 minutes; here is what to do:

(a) Arrange to have all your telephone calls intercepted.

(b) Close your office door.

(c) Take two to three minutes to sweep out the mental debris.

(d) Take a deep breath, grab a pencil, and go!

Let's start with some very basic questions to get you in the right frame of mind.

(a) Why are you even considering a customer relations program?

(b) Why is it essential to your organization?

(c) What do you wish to accomplish?

(d) Are your objectives realistic?

(e) What do you stand to gain?

(f) What do you stand to lose?

(g) Are you willing to commit money to the program?

(h) Do your competitors have a program in place?

(i) What do you admire about their programs?

(j) Are there segments you would wish to plagiarize?

This isn't a complete list. You can add questions of your own, and the more questions you ask, the more you will learn about your organization and your competitors.

The answers you have written down can now be contemplated, verified, then polished, and quickly adopted as your objectives. Once you have cleaned up the prose, you may discover you want to change parts, which is perfectly acceptable.

You may even want to rip the whole thing up and start again, and this is all right too. If you are changing the plan, it means you are thinking about it, and we couldn't ask for anything more.

So remember, your plan is not inscribed in stone...it's a flexible tool to help you recognize some business realities and to guide you in preparing for those realities.

With a good grasp of where you want to go and why you need to go there, next you need to consider the facts about your customers and clients.

e. WHOM ARE YOU TRYING TO REACH?

Your research completed in chapter 4 told you quite a lot about the people who are important to your organization: employees, customers, clients, shareholders, suppliers, and, often, government agencies. Now you need to put a priority on the different groups (for ease of operation) and decide which objectives apply to each. Some objectives may apply only to a limited number of people, while some objectives may be relevant to all groups. It's like mixing and matching your wardrobe. A navy blue jacket can complement light gray slacks in addition to light blue slacks or tan slacks. According to the occasion, you choose one in preference to the other depending on how you wish to appear, what impression you wish to create, and your perception of the group's expectations.

If this principle sounds familiar, it's because you read it in an earlier chapter when we were talking about knowing your organization's image and reputation.

f. BREAKING DOWN THE PLAN

Once you have sliced your research and questions into bite-sized chunks, you then need to slice your plan in a similar fashion — into short-, medium- and long-range goals. It is your plan, so you decide what short-term means to you. It could be one month, one quarter, six months, or a year. It could also be five years for well-established organizations where tradition dictates that change be minimal and gradual.

A useful model that we will use in this book is defining a short range as one year, medium range as three years, and anything five years or more as long range.

In developing your one-year plan, your planning committee or task force should follow these steps:

(a) Determine your organization's weaknesses and potential irritants.

(b) Decide on present strengths and virtues you desire to encourage and add.

(c) Make a commitment to change.

(d) Create and establish a structure that will make the changes more acceptable and easier to implement.

(e) Design clear and precise standards so everyone understands the lines of authority, decision-making powers, and guidelines for behavior.

(f) Develop a system to monitor and evaluate performance. People need to know how well they are doing.

(g) Give top priority to training. Don't assume people will embrace your plans with joy until they understand them and, more important, understand their role in them.

(h) Communicate the progress, or lack of it, continually. Sporadic announcements will receive short shrift. Communication is going to be a major tool in your customer relations program, so why not set an example; show them how to use it, don't just tell them how.

(i) Develop enthusiasm for both the concept and the program. Enthusiasm is contagious. If you don't get wound up about the program possibilities, why should anybody else? The way to develop enthusiasm is by encouraging pride — pride in who a person is, where he or she works, and what he or she produces. Pride is an intangible but powerful ally. We are all familiar with people who exude pride in themselves and their work. They seem to glow and sparkle, and they are literally walking ambassadors for their organizations. With proper encouragement, your people could sparkle and glow considerably brighter.

(j) Determine the rewards for achieving goals and objectives. Announce how the recognition or award will be handled or shared. Also be prepared to recognize outstanding performance by individuals or groups. Again, remind all employees that this is their plan, and it will work only if each takes a personal interest in making it successful.

g. WHO IS GOING TO DO WHAT?

Now you need to bring together all the bits and pieces of paper you have been shuffling and put some names and time frames on them. This is necessary to get people involved and also to get the work done. As an example, Sample #1 shows how one business outlined steps in their recognition/reward system. This type of outline works well for segments of the plan, but for the total plan you need to develop a critical path or flow chart. (See Sample #2.) Use whatever works best for you.

As the pieces of the puzzle start to slip into place we can tentatively put target dates for implementation of program segments on the calendar or critical path. (See Sample #3.)

SAMPLE #1
REWARD/RECOGNITION
PROGRAM FOR XYZ CORPORATION

Committee members	Action needed	Date required	Assigned to	Reporting method
J.D. B.T. F.B. R.H. J.K.	Researching rewards at. ABC Inc.	July 10/8-	B.T. & J.K.	Memo & phone
	Develop monitoring system	Aug. 4/8-	R.H.	Memo Aug. 1 followed by meeting Aug. 5

SAMPLE #2
TASK FORCE TIME TABLE

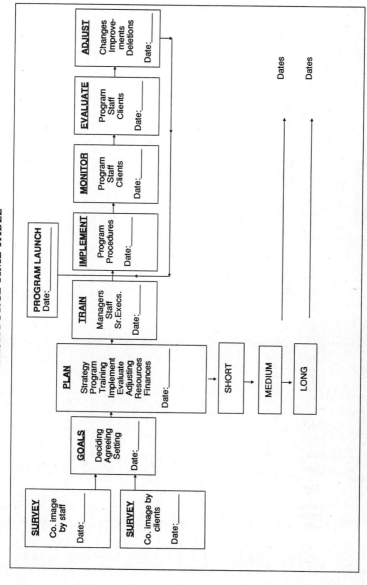

SAMPLE #3
CUSTOMER RELATIONS PROGRAM PLANNING SHEET

	Who is responsible	How will it be done	Start date	Completion date	Approval	Communication methods	Specific concerns	Skill training	Cost (Include release time)
Company image survey: Personnel	J.D.	Staff meeting	May 1	May 30	M.D.	Staff meeting	Morale	J.S.	
Company image survey: Customer/ client	M.S.	Mail	May 1	June 15	M.D.	Staff meeting	Repeat customers	L.M.	
Setting goals									
Planning procedures to meet goals									
* Put on program training here									
Implementing procedures to meet goals Short-term Medium-term Long-term									
Monitoring procedures									
Evaluating procedures									
Adjusting procedures									

h. REVIEW YOUR PLAN

Just about this time you need to pause, step back, and consider what you have accomplished so far. Does it make sense? Is it realistic? Is it what you want?

If the answers are yes, then you need to ask yourself if the plan is put into operation will it affect your quality of service in a negative manner? In other words, will you spend more time fulfilling the plan than in providing quality service to your customers?

Will your service be as good as before, or better, while still being dependable, consistent, time conscious and economical? If the answer comes out yes again, then it's time to buy a large roll of white paper from the stationery suppliers (the type used to cover tables at barbecues), pin a generous length on the wall, and start tracking or developing a king-sized critical path. At this juncture it's relatively simple.

First, at the right edge of the paper write in your implementation date. Next, start working backward slotting in people, activities, time requirements, and deadlines as agreed. The beauty of a big chart is that everybody is aware of it. But even more significant is that people tend to respond more readily when they realize their names, assignments, and completion dates are on public view.

Once you have mastered the one-year plan, repeat the process for the three- and five-year plans. You will find it develops more quickly as the players benefit from the experience of the one-year planning exercise.

i. SUMMARY

In summary, break the large challenge into a series of smaller, more manageable challenges, something everybody can sink their teeth into. Start the process now. Procrastination will make it appear more difficult than it really is. Do it one step at a time. Familiarize yourself with your organization's service in relation to your customers' needs.

Don't try to make a perfect plan. Be willing to scrap it and start over again. It's not wasted time but a valuable learning opportunity, and it lets you acknowledge there could be frills you don't need. Be sure of the impression you wish to develop or enhance. Make certain it's appropriate to you and that you can maintain and improve it indefinitely. Create a workable structure that will ease any change that's necessary. Make sure the program belongs to everybody and everybody is kept informed on progress.

Don't forget the word encouragement. It's the salve for the bruised ego, the vitamin for the tired committee member, and the elixir for continuing success in business.

Share the work, share the accolades, keep to deadlines, keep moving forward.

Unplanned systems operate for the convenience of the organization. Planned systems are for the benefit of customers, clients, and employees. So planning means knowing where you are going and when you expect to arrive. By asking questions, you can develop a customized road map that will chart your intended progress and measure how successful you have been.

CASE STUDY

When the staff meeting was held at The ABC Shoppe, everyone was enthusiastic about the results of their discussions, and a certain pride was evident when they talked about their "fact finding" endeavors. Mary and June offered the following suggestions for improving service to present customers and for attracting new customers:

(a) All customers should be treated as welcome guests with warmth, smiles, and greetings.

(b) Customers should be offered assistance respectfully, but not be harassed or pushed.

(c) If asked for gift suggestions, the salesperson must take the time to be helpful and offer a range of merchandise at varying prices.

(d) New, elegant packaging should be designed and used in a way that would make gift wrapping easy without any additional charge to the customers. Samples and prices were shown.

(e) Customers should be asked if they cared to be placed on a mailing list for upcoming sales and special promotions.

(f) When an item is out of stock, the customer should be asked if he or she wants to be advised when a new shipment comes in. Names and telephone numbers should be entered in a book kept at the sales counter.

(g) Customers, whether they purchase anything or not, should be given a prepaid postcard questionnaire asking for suggestions for better service and ideas for new merchandise. When returned, the postcard would be kept on file and the customer would receive a 10% discount on the next purchase.

(h) Advertising and special promotions should coincide. For example, on Mother's Day a free carnation could be given with every purchase.

(i) Mints, placed in small candy dishes at the front of the store, should be offered to all customers.

(j) Appropriate music should be used as an unobtrusive background.

(k) New marketing ideas should be suggested monthly by employees. When used, the employee should be suitably rewarded.

(l) The customer must be given full, discreet attention. When a customer enters the store, the employees must stop doing whatever they are busy with and help the customer.

(m) All staff, regardless of title, must treat each other with respect.

(n) A shopper's service for people who cannot do their own shopping should be implemented. The store could keep on file details about preferences of price ranges, individual taste in colors and styles, and the selection, gift wrapping, and delivery would be provided at no extra charge.

(o) A gift suggestion catalogue should be mailed to businesses in the area promoting the shopper's service for retirement gifts or personalized recognition awards.

(p) A calendar of special days should be kept for busy customers to remind them in advance of birthdays and anniversaries. The reminder could include sizes, special requirements, and a tasteful list of suggestions.

(q) Flowers could be ordered as an added service (from the shop next door) and unusual gifts could be suggested. While these would not represent direct sales of merchandise, each transaction would build trust between the customer and the store and would establish the dependability of the store for assistance with a variety of needs.

Mary and June summarized by noting that it is important to measure the responses to flyers, catalogues, special days, and special events so that they know what works and what doesn't. A simple question to the customer, "How did you find out about our special?" would provide the answer, which must be recorded to provide a meaningful measurement of responses.

Jim and April, as predicted, came up with a detailed plan for employee evaluation and training. Using the responses from customers, employers, and employees, they were able to complete the plan. It is shown in Sample #4.

John's report consisted of the need for a checklist for opening the store. He presented part of it and asked for contributions from the staff. It took shape along these lines:

(a) Arrive no later than 8:30 a.m. Store must be opened promptly at 9:00 a.m.

(b) Before store is opened —

- Turn on all lights
- Clean counter, window, and mirrors
- Tidy displays
- Count cash float

There was also a checklist for the person who closed the store, another for dealing with suppliers, marking and pricing, and stocking the shelves.

The result of the task forces was the evolution of a customer service program that kept the focus firmly on the customer. It began with an orderly, logical way of doing business and a demonstrated concern for personnel development, and it provided the foundation for a continuing program to better serve the customers. Best of all, because everyone had been involved and each had contributed, it become "our" plan for "our" store.

The results of the task forces and surveys showed a definite need for training and employee recognition, plus some role changes for everyone but June, who continued in her job as clerk.

Mary gave her bookkeeping chores to Jim and took over one of his evenings and some of his Saturdays in the store. This gave her some first-hand ideas about what customers wanted in the way of merchandise and helped her buy stock with customers' preferences in mind.

April took the responsibilities of dealing with the suppliers, pricing inventory, and arranging displays. John, alone, would be the boss.

Samples #5 and #6 show the planning and implementation process for The ABC Shoppe.

SAMPLE #4
THE ABC CUSTOMER RELATIONS PROGRAM
SKILL EVALUATION

To be filled in by *all* employees   (designed by Jim and April)

STAFF	AREAS FOR IMPROVEMENT	AREAS OF STRENGTH	POTENTIAL VIRTUES	APPEARANCE AND BEHAVIOR GUIDELINES
JOHN	Managerial skills Getting used to authority Negotiating skills Understanding of publicity	People skills Enthusiasm Attention to detail Dependable	Motivational skills Positive attitude Leadership qualities	Must look like leader Must act like leader Must dress like leader
MARY	Not sales oriented Too consumer-oriented Unused to business conversation Never had to promote business	Good buying instincts Has people skills Confident in abilities	Objective view of staff Analytical view of businesss Orderly mind for long-range planning	Good appearance Looks successful Needs to develop confidence in skills
JUNE	Poor "dress" image Student Almost too popular Too much "slang"	Good personality, warm and friendly; seems genuinely interested in customers Outgoing, enthusiastic Willing to learn	Friendliness could encourage customers to return if proper relationship established Attracts young clientele	Dress unacceptable Needs advice on clothing and language
JIM	Almost too businesslike Uses a minimum of words and appears abrupt Shyness is part of problem	Good, methodical mind Persistent Works hard Has good business background	Bookkeeping skills could be utilized more often Could be valuable in dealing with senior execs or business organizations	Dresses rather stodgy, although good quality Needs more modern wardrobe attitude
APRIL	Brusque with customers Defensive, fault-finding Poor people skills	Excellent displays Thorough in marking and stocking A lot of determination Appropriate dress	Artistic talent a big plus in attracting clients May have skills in haute couture not realized	Appearance is good, but dealings with customers poor Etiquette needs work

SAMPLE #4 — Continued

STAFF	DESIRED STANDARDS	PERFORMANCE EVALUATION	REWARDS AVAILABLE	TRAINING NEEDED
JOHN	To be a leader Exhibit confidence Encourage others Make sound decisions		Increased income from more successful store	Leadership skills Managing people Strategic planning Promotion and publicity
MARY	To be able to fill in as boss, and exhibit managerial skills as well as sales skills		Increased income from more successful store	Sales training Some leadership skills
JUNE	Personal goals are set in conjunction with Mary then by John	Evaluated initially by Mary then reviewed by John	Rewards should be equally available to all employees: • A profit-sharing plan • Monetary rewards for achieving sales goals	Sales training Image awareness Etiquette training
JIM	Personal goals are set in conjunction with Mary then approved by John	Evaluated initially by Mary then reviewed by John	• Suggestion box — if used • Cost-cutting ideas • Labor saving ideas	Sales training Image awareness Confidence building Etiquette training
APRIL	Personal goals are set in conjunction with Mary then approved by John	Evaluated initially by Mary then reviewed by John		Sales training Image awareness Communication skills Courtesy and politeness

THE ABC CUSTOMER RELATIONS PROGRAM PLANNING FLOWCHART

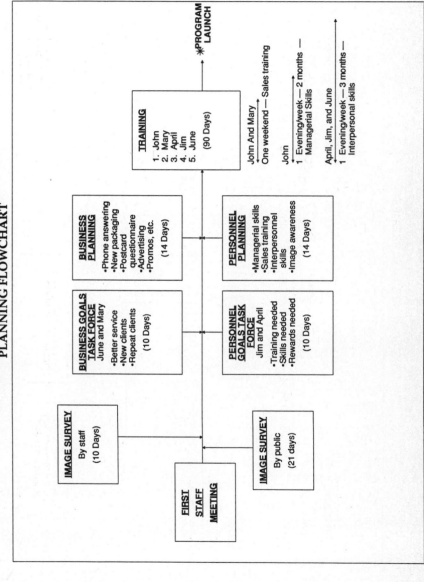

IMAGE SURVEY
By staff
(10 Days)

FIRST STAFF MEETING

IMAGE SURVEY
By public
(21 days)

BUSINESS GOALS TASK FORCE
June and Mary
•Better service
•New clients
•Repeat clients
(10 Days)

BUSINESS PLANNING
•Phone answering
•New packaging
•Postcard questionnaire
•Advertising
•Promos, etc.
(14 Days)

PERSONNEL GOALS TASK FORCE
Jim and April
•Training needed
•Skills needed
•Rewards needed
(10 Days)

PERSONNEL PLANNING
•Managerial skills
•Sales training
•Interpersonnel skills
•Image awareness
(14 Days)

TRAINING
1. John
2. Mary
3. April
4. Jim
5. June
(90 Days)

✳ PROGRAM LAUNCH

John And Mary
One weekend — Sales training

John
1 Evening/week — 2 months —
Managerial Skills

April, Jim, and June
1 Evening/week — 3 months —
Interpersonal skills

69

SAMPLE #6
THE ABC CUSTOMER RELATIONS PROGRAM
IMPLEMENTATION PROCESS

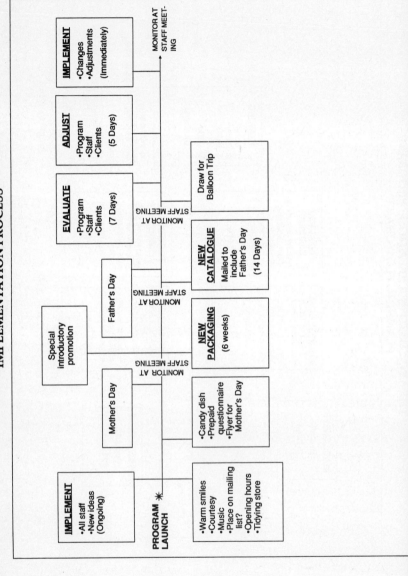

7

COMMUNICATING YOUR CUSTOMER RELATIONS PROGRAM TO YOUR EMPLOYEES

Good customer relations begins with good employee relations. Both you and your staff must be sold on the program; as managers and supervisors know, you get work done through your staff. Being able to communicate effectively with employees can mean the difference between the success or failure of your customer relations program and, ultimately, your business. Throughout this book, we've emphasized communication as being always important to the plan. Now it is time to be specific.

a. COMMUNICATING WITH EMPLOYEES

Frequently, too much attention is paid to the way we communicate, and not enough to content and purpose. We become engrossed with memos and meetings, forgetting that communication is taking place all the time during every minute of the job. Good communication cannot be switched on and off at somebody's whim. Nor is communication a placebo or gimmick to be used at a time of crisis or when promoting a new program. Good communication is the heart of any business, the most important tool for getting things done. It is the basis for understanding, for cooperation, for action...and for profit.

Communicating with your staff is not accomplished by words alone. Tone of voice, facial expressions, the set of the shoulders, the lift of an eyebrow — all send a message that is

71

read by employees. Even silence sends a message; we can all recall the words that were not said, either in praise or rebuke. An owner, manager, or supervisor casts a long shadow; each word or action is larger than life to an employee. The employee, whether reacting or emulating, in turn casts a shadow on the customer or client.

b. ESSENTIALS OF GOOD EMPLOYEE COMMUNICATION

Communication is a journey, not a destination. It isn't the single step of transmitting an idea — telling someone. Good communication begins with listening — being sincerely concerned about people and their problems and becoming enthusiastic about their ideas.

The second step in good communication is thinking through and clarifying an idea in your own mind, then with the help of others, setting a purpose for the communication. The third step is to share the idea with the people who will carry it out, and the fourth step is to share your enthusiasm for the idea and get your people energized to take the action that will fulfill the purpose of the communication. The final step is follow-through; you need to monitor the process, and the results, to see if the action is ongoing and unchanging.

Let's take a look at those steps and see if they tie into your customer relations program.

1. Listening

Your listening began when you asked for input from your employees. You listened carefully to their concerns and their ideas for the program. You took what they had to say seriously, sometimes compromising your own ideas when you realized that their's made more sense.

2. Purpose

Having taken into consideration the company's objectives, your own goals, and the input from your employees, you built a customer relations program. Your purpose is to convince the employees to put the program into practice and make it work.

3. Communicating the idea

This step is not as simple as it may seem. The message must be sent in a language that employees can understand. Too often employee reaction to a "state-of-the-union" message by the company president is "What was that all about?" The message has not been delivered in language that the audience understands or relates to, or the message is not complete.

A whole department in a Calgary-based oil company became disgruntled when the company moved into a new multi-million dollar building. The department's perception was that it was getting less space than in the old building. In fact, they were getting more space. Someone neglected to tell them that they had additional storage space on another floor. Less space translated into loss of prestige. The ensuing dissatisfaction was expressed in a work-to-rule attitude that became so evident the company president got involved and started an enquiry into the problem.

Good communicators keep their antennas tuned in. They develop a sensitivity to both the viewpoint and the level of comprehension of their staff. They realize an employee receives a message, whether written or verbal, and thinks "How will this affect me? Does it mean more or less money? More work? A change in status? Longer hours?"

Before you talk with your staff about your new customer relations program, be sure you think through your method of communicating. Think through, too, how they will react to your proposal.

4. Motivating personnel

Not only must you have a purpose for your communication, be sensitive to your personnel, and express your ideas with clarity, but you must also encourage your people to accept the new ideas, and then act on them. Employees respond better when they know what is expected of them, when they learn about change before it takes place, and when they feel free to discuss problems with supervisors. When they believe they are an important part of the organization, they will work with greater interest and enthusiasm. It's the working and communicating relationship between management, supervisors, and employees on a daily basis that builds a team. As trust develops, the quality of the working-communicating relationship improves and in turn motivates that team. Motivation comes from within. Neither flowery speeches nor negative haranguing will motivate personnel.

A store manager addressed his staff by bawling them out for an hour and a half. He called them down for their past performance, made comparisons between staff members, and generally painted a black picture of the retail business in general. He concluded with threats of firing if sales did not improve. Then he asked for questions and comments. A newly hired employee spoke: "You have certainly given us all the negatives of the business. Are there any good reasons why we should be working in this business, and particularly for you?" The manager was dumbfounded by the question and could not think of one positive thing to say. The outcome was that three employees quit. Customers were confronted by either fearful or defensive sales staff and sales did not go up. The store manager had not created a positively motivated team. He did not listen, he did not inspire, he did not set a good example.

Employees see economic benefits, more money, and more security as reasons to do a good job. But they desperately need recognition for a job well done plus a measure of personal job satisfaction. They need the regard of managers and supervisors along with fellow employees. Many would like the opportunity to take on more responsibility. When you present your customer relations plan to your employees, be aware that encouragement is a vehicle that will motivate them, so they can plan their part in the program willingly and with purpose.

5. Following through

Telling personnel about your customer relations plan is just the beginning. Every communication must have a follow-through. Your well-thought-out plan has steps that need to be followed in sequence. Each step has a monitoring point to see that the agreed procedure has been followed, and is built into the plan. The prime consideration is making sure that your staff completely understands the plan. You must ensure that all the steps and evaluations take place just as outlined in the plan. As in the game of golf, if there is no follow-through in your swing, your plan will start to go off course.

c. COMMUNICATION MUST BE CONSTANT

In the long run, employees are motivated by what management does, not by what it says. Nobody is fooled by the manager who suddenly becomes concerned over your health or your son's baseball team when previously a grunt was all you got in reply to your "good morning." Communication grows in a climate of trust and confidence. The supervisor-manager who keeps promises, reports facts honestly, and listens sincerely does not have to fall back on phony good fellowship. Before you "sell" your customer relations program to your staff, assess your own communication skills and make a determined effort to upgrade those that need polishing, particularly if you expect your message to be understood, accepted, and properly introduced.

Ask yourself these questions:

(a) If I make a promise, do I follow through?

(b) If I am asked for help or information, do I listen and respond sincerely, without sarcasm or criticism?

(c) If I ask for input, do I listen with genuine interest and use the input whenever possible?

(d) Do I credit the person's input?

(e) Do I give praise when it is due? (But not use insincere flattery to create good will?)

(f) Do I ask questions when I don't understand?

(g) Do I stimulate people to ask questions and express their ideas?

If you can answer yes to these questions, then it's time to launch your customer relations plan with your staff. But if you have not created a good communications climate, it's critical you spend some time doing so before you present your plan. (You may wish to have others evaluate you using the above questions. Sometimes a person's own perception is biased.)

CASE STUDY

From the surveys, John found that he was a good listener. As a journalist, he was trained to gather information. Mary, as a dentist, usually spent time with people who had their mouths full of cotton. She was used to telling patients what to do and found she was an impatient listener wanting to "get on with it." As professionals, both worked hard at keeping their promises and were used to meeting deadlines. They found themselves weak when it came to giving praise. As strong individuals often working alone, they did not expect or need a great deal of praise themselves.

It was also a revelation when they realized that rarely had they asked for input from the staff. The staff concurred with their self-evaluation. With the decision that the store should have only one boss, and that should be John who spent more time in the store than Mary, the answers helped them make a conscious decision to keep their partnership discussions away from the store.

d. GETTING YOUR IDEAS ACROSS

Getting ideas across makes up more than 50% of the working day of executives, managers, and supervisors. Hicks B. Waldron, Chairman and CEO of Avon Products Inc., says that he spends 60% of his time communicating. The largest part of that time is communicating to employees ranging from hourly workers to senior managers. His communication is aimed at rallying employees to support company plans in order to improve business.

When you present new ideas to employees, present them in small chunks and in simple language. Decide beforehand what your thrust is. In the case of your customer relations communication it is the whole plan. The second thing to decide is what the main parts of the plan are and finally what details the staff need to understand the whole idea. Often, too many details are presented too soon, which can confuse everyone. Be patient with the listener who is slow to grasp your points. Take time to explain, but not at the expense of others. Offer to discuss their concerns on an individual basis.

e. ORDERS

Orders differ from ideas. Ideas can prompt discussion and can be changed. An order is given to bring about certain results. Orders can fall into three general classifications:

(a) The implied order or suggestion that something needs to be done but leaves the doer to go ahead on his or her own initiative

(b) The request — a mild, tactful form of order. "How would you like to..." or "I wonder if you would...."

(c) The direct order, straightforward command: "Do this," "Don't do that."

A request does not offend the sensitive worker. The first time an error is made, a request to correct it adds the friendliness that keeps the employee on your side. The direct order

77

may have to be used if the error is repeated. An emergency is another occasion that usually requires a direct order, which when used infrequently, stands out emphatically.

The presentation of your customer relations program should not be an order. If your plan has been conceived with proper input from your staff, the presentation should prompt discussion but little change for acceptance. You may find, however, that as the plan goes into practice and becomes a concrete policy, you may want strict adherence to it. Reminders, requests, and suggestions should be used before resorting to orders. Orders should be given in private if possible. They may be necessary to avert a crisis or to shock workers and ultimately save them from dismissal.

1. **Requisites for giving orders**

(a) The employee receiving the order must have the training, skill, and physical ability to carry out the order satisfactorily.

(b) The employee should understand how the order fits into the total context.

(c) The employee should carry out the order willingly. This is usually the direct result of the manner, including tone of voice, in which the order is given.

(d) The order should be made important in the mind of the employees carrying it out. Orders, suggestions, or requests that are merely "thrown out" will be carried out in the same manner.

(e) Make an order perfectly clear: what the employee is to do, how it is to be done, when it is to be done, and the result expected. Speak the language the employee understands. Remember, just because the employee nods in agreement does not mean the message has been understood.

2. Giving orders

(a) Point out the facts or conditions that have made the order necessary. You want to dispel any impression that the order is a personal reprimand.

(b) State the results expected.

(c) Thoroughly understand the job to be done yourself.

(d) Assign work to the proper employee.

(e) Give the orders clearly, concisely, and distinctly.

(f) Don't assume the orders are understood; be sure they are understood. Ask for feedback.

(g) Avoid sarcasm and profanity.

(h) Do not give an order in anger.

(i) If possible, demonstrate.

(j) Do not give too many orders at one time.

(k) Give orders through proper channels. Do not bypass an immediate supervisor to order an employee.

(l) Some orders should be written down. Directions and company policies are good examples. Keep the language simple. For example, saying "Refrain from engaging" instead of "don't" is a waste of words.

(m) Follow through. Check back to be sure that the employee has understood and is performing the order satisfactorily.

(n) Praise, sincerely, when it is due.

f. REPRIMANDING

Good customer relations must be consistent. If an employee communicates negatively with clients and customers, immediate action is needed by the manager or supervisor to communicate the problem to the staff member and to change behavior. Once your customer relations plan has been communicated to your employees, accepted by them, and in place, it must be operational at all times. One non-performing employee can undermine the whole program.

Before you reprimand, get all the facts first. The customer who reports poor service may be a constant complainer. Know your employees well. If you have created the right working atmosphere with employees who are conscientious, you know they take pride in their jobs and in their company.

Never lose your temper and bawl out an employee and never reprimand an employee in front of others. You only lose your own credibility. Keep your composure and logically discuss the problem and the consequences of the employee's actions.

Listen carefully and calmly. Ask what could have caused the incident: worry, indifference, health, misunderstanding, resentment, no commitment to the program? Use a sympathetic, interested approach. Don't let prejudice or bias interfere with the process.

The employee should understand what the problem is, how he or she created the problem, what the consequences are, what is to be done, and what to expect if the problem occurs again. Make the employee understand what effect the incident has on the company, on fellow employees, and on him or herself.

Get the employee to take responsibility for his or her future conduct. You want a loyal, enthusiastic, dependable employee willing to cooperate and make your customer relations plan work.

g. SUMMARY

(a) Listen to your employees both when planning and communicating the program and at every step of its implementation:

(i) Make the physical setting conducive to good listening. Make it private and get rid of distractions like ringing phones and curious onlookers.

(ii) Face the person squarely so you can take in not only what they are saying, but how they are saying it.

(iii) Rid yourself of bias and prejudice.

(iv) If the person is reluctant to talk, ask questions. Express what you feel. Find out if they share the same opinion.

(v) Interrupt sparingly. Do not contradict.

(vi) Do not lose your temper. Hear the other person out.

(vii) If the other person loses his or her temper, let him or her talk and defuse.

(viii) Listen for ideas and underlying feelings.

(ix) Consider the other person's point of view.

(x) Evaluate fairly the logic and credibility of what you hear.

(xi) Do not feel you must have the last word.

(b) When you present your customer relations plan, set goals:

(i) Set your immediate goal.

(ii) Set your long-term goals.

(iii) Break down your information into small pieces. Use only as much detail as is necessary.

(c) Know your employees:

(i) What is their present attitude toward work, the company, yourself?

(ii) What do they expect from you? (Leadership and direction)

(iii) Will they see the plan as something worthwhile to themselves, or only something worthwhile to you?

(d) Know yourself: If your communication habits are bad, you should be implementing change before you present your plan. If necessary, take a course or get some individual coaching. You want to sell your plan and be credible.

(e) Plan your approach:

   (i) Choose the right time. You may wish to conform to the custom of meeting Monday morning, or you may wish to make the presentation of the plan a very special event. Once again, be aware of employees sensibilities. Don't keep them in the dark. One large Canadian petroleum company made it a practice to fire personnel after they had returned from vacation. It got so that no one would take their scheduled vacation period because they were afraid they would be without a job on return. Let employees know what the meeting is about and that it is good news.

   (ii) Consult with others. Keep an ongoing dialogue with those who played an active part in the planning process. Get them involved in the presentation of the plan.

   (iii) Choose a location that allows for the right atmosphere.

   (iv) Be natural, but serious in your delivery style. Judge their reaction to a positive or negative approach. "We've got real trouble with your customer services" or "We've got the answer to our customer relations problem."

   (v) Keep it simple. Don't try to discuss too much at one time. Speak in language everyone understands.

   (vi) Allow for discussion.

82

(vii) Answer questions clearly.

(viii) Follow through. Have procedures that will get the plan off and running and use them. Have a method of evaluating long-term procedures at various points. Evaluate the success of the procedures at appropriate conclusions.

(ix) Be prepared to give credit.

(x) Be prepared to turn your plan into policy, policy into procedure, and procedure into orders.

(xi) Be prepared to reward or reprimand, fairly.

CASE STUDY

At The ABC Shoppe, John and Mary were able to build a team by truly participating in the staff meetings and in the task forces, and by really listening and responding to their staff.

John found that he usually only had to request, or even suggest, a point, and soon the work was done. Only on one occasion did he have to reprimand. April had just finished putting together a very attractive display when a customer removed the cashmere sweater to have a better look at it. April, feeling miffed, her masterpiece having been dismantled, told the customer not to touch the display. John made light of the moment and while the customer did not buy that particular sweater, she bought another. In the privacy of his office, John reminded April that while she had to redo the display, she should keep in mind that the objective was to sell the merchandise. He also reminded her that she would be sharing in the commission from the sale.

8
TRAINING EMPLOYEES

We said in chapter 1 that a problem with customer service is that employees are not encouraged to think nor are they trained for responsibility. To ensure the success of your customer relations program, make sure all employees feel they have a stake in its success. Find ways to get them involved and enthused. Remind them that this is their program.

Once you have agreed on the objectives for your program, it's a good idea to include training in your plans. Telephone answering techniques, sales procedures, dress and decorum may need sprucing up, so include them from the outset.

You can organize and present the training program yourself or use consultants. Either way it's important that training not be confused with function. Keep it separate from regularly scheduled work.

Training must not be used to evaluate an employee's work performance. Imagine our dismay on finding a supervisor in one of our training workshops using the performance of participants as part of their job evaluation. Imagine, also, their reaction if they know they are being evaluated while struggling to master new and unfamiliar skills. Obviously they would recoil from being involved. Your employees would react in a similar manner and your whole customer relations program could be stranded before it even has a chance to get airborne. Let us repeat: Do not use the learning process as foundation for job appraisal. Later, as the workers become more comfortable with the new skills and start to use them on the job, then, and only then, may they be evaluated.

Training should be ongoing. As your program becomes a part of the company's process of doing business, it should be a regularly scheduled component of that process to train new personnel and to revitalize and update skills of longtime employees.

a. PREPARATION FOR TRAINING

1. Prepare a training plan

(a) Once you have completed your customer relations plan, go over it carefully to pinpoint areas where new employee skills are needed to make the plan work.

(b) All instruction should meet certain definite needs. Don't try to cover everything in one session.

(c) Decide who should receive the training. Only those needing the instruction should take part. We have conducted too many seminars where employees are there merely to pass the time for they will never be using the skills presented.

(d) Attendance at the seminar should be introduced to employees as an opportunity, not as a reprimand or criticism of their performance or lack of skill.

2. Prepare a breakdown of the job or process

Whether you are conducting the training sessions yourself or using outside consultants, you need to have a clearly thought out, logical method of instruction. If you are engaging consultants, check that they have a clearly planned curriculum, but one that is flexible enough to meet the changing needs of your business and your employees. Go over their material with them to see if their plans are well organized and if their methods and materials will meet the training objectives you have set.

(a) Training materials should concentrate on the important steps and key points to be learned.

(b) All steps or points should be clearly illustrated and demonstrated by the trainer.

(c) Details should be carefully selected and used only to emphasize and support the steps or points.

(d) Include any short cuts or knacks you can pass on that will help employees understand or perform new tasks or new skills.

3. Have everything ready for the training session

(a) Employees should know exactly what day, time, and place the training will take place. Make the training session important; give it meaning. People cannot do their jobs and attend a training session at the same time. Give them the time to attend, even if this means training at a hotel or training center.

(b) Keep numbers small so everyone can participate.

(c) The room, materials, and equipment should all be ready and functional before training begins. Poorly prepared instructors and equipment that doesn't work create a very poor impression.

(d) Start every session on time. This sets the tone for training and underlines its importance.

b. STEPS IN INSTRUCTING

1. Prepare the employee for instruction

(a) Put the employee at ease. In no way should employees feel they are being tested or reprimanded for poor performance. We reiterate, training should be looked upon as a career opportunity to make work easier and more effective.

(b) Explain the training and its importance both to the employee and to the company. Explain its importance to the total customer relations plan.

(c) Create an interest. Employee involvement in creating the customer relations plan should have created interest in the training. Reinforce what the success of the total program will mean to the individual employee.

2. Present the training — show and tell

(a) The trainer should follow the sequence of the new task or the process.

(b) Explain or demonstrate one step at a time.

(c) Stress key points. How it is done, why it is done, why it should be done a certain way and not another. Don't waste time on unimportant details.

(d) Don't tell too much at one time. Stick to the facts. Repeat important details.

(e) Use simple language. Plain talk gets your message across best, but don't "talk down."

(f) Allow discussion.

(g) Allow participation — hands on rather than observation of the trainer.

(h) Break into groups for problem solving and role playing. Employees can emulate customers with ease and some acting talent!

(i) Set a high standard for the trainer's performance whether it is you or a consultant. If you are telling employees to be courteous and helpful to customers, but not demonstrating those qualities in your training sessions, your employees will react negatively.

Trainers set the standard, not only for their own performances, but for that of the participants.

(j) Give reasons for methods and procedures. Rationale is important. The "why" and the "how" should be explained clearly.

(k) Show, demonstrate, teach one thing at a time. If part of your new customer relations plan is to get customers to be on a mailing list, do not try to initiate this procedure with new employees until they have firmly grasped how to write the receipt, fill out a charge card slip, and handle returns. Add the new procedure once they have the routine of making the sale well in hand. A confused employee signals a confused business to a customer.

3. Try out the performance

(a) Have the employee do the job or follow the procedure. If possible have the employee do it in front of the full group or for a small group. But whatever the method, make sure everyone involved in the training session gets to "do the job" during training. Praise and build confidence.

(b) Have the participants explain the key points of the job or procedures. This can be done while demonstrating in front of the total group or in small groups. This will assure you that your material, procedures, and skills have been grasped by the participants.

4. Correcting errors or omissions

(a) Compliment before you correct.

(b) Do not belittle or be sarcastic.

(c) Build on the strengths demonstrated by the participant.

(d) Let the participant correct himself or herself.

(e) If possible do not correct in front of others. If you must, make the correction a general reminder for everyone.

(f) Don't be too quick to correct. The fault may lie with the trainer. Go over the information or procedure again for everyone's benefit.

5. Encourage participants

(a) Give sincere compliments.

(b) Thank them for good ideas.

(c) Be prompt with compliments.

6. Make sure participants have a complete understanding of the process, procedure or skill

(a) If the employee seems to be slow in comprehension arrange for individual consultation or more training.

7. Follow through

(a) Put the employees on their own when you are satisfied they have the confidence and knowledge to complete the job, follow the procedure, or apply the new skills.

(b) Encourage more discussion and further questions — your door remains open.

(c) Check frequently, but gradually taper off as you see confidence growing and ability improving.

(d) Let employees know they are doing a good job. Your total customer relations plan has a method of measuring whether or not it is working. Newly acquired skills will either make the plan a success or failure. If there is need to further improve skills, say so. It is your responsibility to let employees know when they are doing a job correctly and also to let them know when improvement is called for.

(e) After a (designated) mutually agreed time, assess the total results of the training in respect to your customer relations program. Determine whether more training is necessary, if the principles need review or if other employees should have similar training.

c. SUMMARY

Your new customer relations program may not work unless your employees receive some very specific training. Determine what that training should be, who should receive it, and who should teach it. Sell the training to your employees as an opportunity for growth for them and the organization. Training should not be seen as a punishment or criticism. Know exactly what it is you want the training to accomplish, what you want the participants to learn, and how they will apply those skills to their jobs. More important, show how the training will benefit your customer relations program over the long haul. Set aside time for the training. Create a learning environment. Keep the training procedures simple. Be sure everyone participates in the training and demonstrates their new skills or knowledge. Follow through. Skills need to be applied and then evaluated: Did the training have value? Did it make a difference to your customer relations success? And remember, training should produce living, breathing, thinking people who can function individually and pleasantly during the best of times, during depression, or during crisis.

CASE STUDY

Information from their customer surveys, the task forces, and staff discussion indicated that there was a need for training for the owners and employees of The ABC Shoppe. And it was with a sense of anticipation that they all agreed to work on improving their personal skills. Areas for immediate attention were —

(a) Sales training for everyone

(b) Managerial skills for John

(c) Interpersonal skills for April

(d) Personal image help for June

Also, a weekend sales training program was offered by a consulting company with a sound international reputation. John and Mary made an executive decision, and with a couple of weeks' notice to the public, closed the store for the weekend. They subsequently agreed the loss in revenue was compensated by the gain in knowledge. They were able to monitor the success of the training by implementing the skills learned and the results that followed. Even more rewarding, they found their customers favorable to the idea of personnel training.

John was able to get his managerial training one evening a week over a two-month period at the local community college. He shared his enthusiasm for his new found knowledge with Mary and the rest of the staff at their weekly meeting.

Not wanting to isolate April, Jim and June joined her one evening a week at the community college for a course on interpersonal skills. All three found the course rewarding. Jim became less brusque and his attitude mellowed; June tempered her bubbly outbursts and channeled her natural enthusiasm toward getting the customer enthused. And, most important, April discovered the image she projected to the world was a facade to make up for what she felt were her inadequacies. Video-taped role playing showed the differences between a smile and a frown, the tone and influence of the voice, the overuse of slang and negative body language. Jim, June, and April became very supportive of each other and the team spirit was encouraged by John and Mary.

Finally, one store meeting focussed on personal image — what would best reflect the store's image of quality and prestige. Mary arranged for a friend who was an image and color consultant to speak informally. She also arranged for personal consultation for each staff member, herself, and the consultant. The result was that the entire staff benefited and Mary and April spent an evening in a quality consignment store putting together a "store wardrobe" for June. The cost was less than one-third of what it would have cost originally. The basic four pieces, two blouses, and two skirts translated into four different outfits, or eight when accessorized. June stayed within her limited budget while the quality image of the store's sales staff remained consistent.

9
BRINGING IT ALL TOGETHER

Now that you have read through the preceding chapters, here is a quick review.

a. THE CUSTOMER RELATIONS PROGRAM

Figure #2 on the next page shows the cycle of steps in a successful customer relations program:

(a) Begin with research: Your image as perceived by yourself. Your image as perceived by customers.

(b) Set goals: What you want your image and reputation to be.

(c) Training: Preparing staff to handle new responsibilities and become familiar with the program.

(d) Implement procedures: Take steps to make goals a reality.

(e) Monitor: Set in place methods to determine whether steps are being followed.

(f) Evaluate: Determine if the procedures are getting the results to achieve your goals.

(g) Adjust: Be prepared to make changes.

(h) Communication and skill training: Ongoing at every step of the process.

FIGURE # 2
CUSTOMER RELATIONS CYCLE

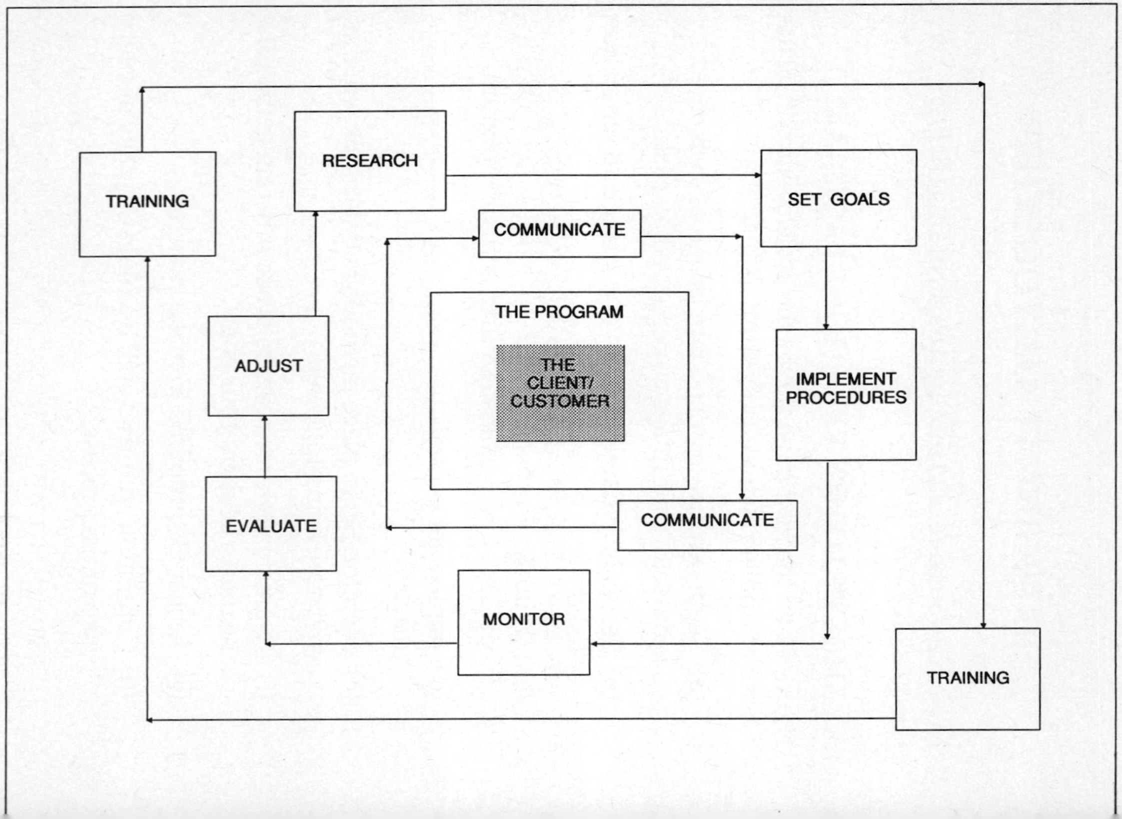

b. DESIGNING YOUR CRITICAL PATH

1. Set goals for your business

(a) Identify what the image of your business is at the present time as perceived by you, your people, and your customers. This can be done through questionnaires, meetings, one-on-one conversations, and telephone calls. Make sure everyone is asked the same questions so that you are able to use and compare fairly the information received.

(b) Determine what you want the image of your business to be.

(c) Determine what must be changed, compromised, or added to turn that image into a reality.

2. Plan to reach your goals

(a) Set down your goals as determined in Step 1.

(b) Give them a priority.

(c) Determine if one is dependent upon another.

(d) Determine your short-range, medium-range, and long-range goals.

3. Determine your strategy

(a) Determine how each goal can be achieved. Does it mean changing or eliminating an existing procedure, introducing a new procedure, or introducing a training program? You may want to appoint a task force of employees to study how a goal could be achieved.

(b) Establish a time frame for their discussion, for reporting back, and for introduction of their report to the rest of your staff for discussion, acceptance, modification, or rejection. You could have a task force for each goal. The more your employees can be involved the more they become a part of the success of the program.

4. Monitor progress and success

Once you have established the methods needed to reach your goals, you must establish a way to monitor the progress and success of each goal. This method could be determined by the task force that established the program for achievement, or it could evolve from employee discussion following the agreement on procedure. Whatever the method, it must be acceptable to the employees.

You may consider customer surveys through questionnaires or telephone interviews, monitoring of employees' performance through an agreed upon procedure, or feedback from employees at regularly designated intervals.

5. Set time frames

Setting a time frame tells people you mean business. Deadlines also get the adrenalin flowing, giving you the extra energy and motivation to get cracking. Chapter 6 discussed putting names and dates to actions that need to take place; when all task force members have a current flow chart that specifies people, places, and progress it's surprising how well people respond to their responsibilities.

6. Implement your program

There must be no surprises. Everybody must be kept updated. It takes only one employee to sarcastically ask "They're doing what today?" to cast doubt on the veracity of the program. If the program has been well planned and if everybody has been kept informed, a launch date will create excitement and anticipation as your business "family" eagerly awaits the birth of their latest offspring.

7. Monitor progress

Once launched, the program must be monitored at the times and dates agreed upon. Delay leads to further delay and frustration for those who are keeping their part of the bargain. Timely monitoring prevents problems from festering

96

from neglect and will send a signal to your customers that you mean what you say.

8. Reassess and adjust

Timely monitoring will also encourage prompt adjustments and necessary changes. The longer a problem prevails, the harder it becomes to change or improve it; it becomes entrenched.

9. Set new goals if desired

Be ready to change some goals and objectives if your evaluation proves them to be questionable or only marginal. There's no disgrace in admitting an idea didn't work; in fact it's a sign of maturity and business acumen to recognize a problem early and correct it before damage can ensue. After all, isn't business all about profiting from our mistakes?

c. THE BOTTOM LINE — MEASURING THE SUCCESS OF YOUR CUSTOMER RELATIONS PROGRAM

This is where you bring it all together and see if your bottom line makes sense. The chart on the next page will help you do this. Alternatively, you may wish to design your own chart for measuring your program's success.

Now answer these questions —

(a) Have overall sales increased above traditional or seasonal growth?

(b) Have profits increased?

(c) Has the regular customer base decreased?

(d) Has the regular customer base increased its buying?

(e) Has the number of new customers increased?

(f) Have new customers become repeats?

(g) Are satisfied customers referring others?

	Average at intro of program	3 mos. later	6 mos. later	1 yr. later	% over-head
Revenue					
Profit					
Customer base					
Repeat customer base					
New customers					
Repeat of new customers					
Customers referred by established customers					
Employee base					
Employee resignations					
Cost of training					

(h) Has the employee base increased or decreased? (If it has decreased, is your operation more efficient? If it has increased, has it been to provide better service?)

(i) Have employee resignations increased or decreased?

(j) Has the program given employees pride and recognition?

(k) Has the cost of training been defrayed by an increase in revenue or has it not been justified?

CASE STUDY

This is a good point to summarize the study of The ABC Shoppe. Over a period of six months, the store increased both its client base and its sales. Profits went up 23%. John and Mary found that 46% of their increase in sales could be traced directly to repeat customers. They also discovered that 35% of their new customers were direct referrals from satisfied customers. They had had no resignations, although they realized they may soon have to replace June who would be graduating from university in six months. But they had a bonus because she agreed to help them find her own replacement when the time came. As she says, she doesn't want just anyone working in "her store."

The cost for training was under $2,000 and there may be further costs when they get their new computer installed. But, in retrospect, $2,000 a year seems a small sum to pay to keep profits climbing, customers satisfied, staff up to date, and to maintain unlimited potential for continuing growth and success.

TITLES AVAILABLE
FROM
SELF-COUNSEL PRESS

BUSINESS TITLES

ASSERTIVENESS FOR MANAGERS
Valuable advice for anyone in a supervisory position is given on effective skills for managing people. Exercises are included.

BASIC ACCOUNTING FOR THE SMALL BUSINESS
Discusses day-to-day accounting problems encountered in running a small business. Instructions for preliminary bookkeeping and organizing financial matters are given.

BE A BETTER MANAGER
From effective speaking to appraising people, to trouble shooting and to budgeting, all the required management skills and techniques are treated clearly and concisely, and arranged by topic in alphabetical order for easy reference.

BUSINESS GUIDE TO EFFECTIVE SPEAKING
This book provides a straightforward approach to developing and improving on-the-job speaking skills, with an emphasis on media techniques, and the new technologies of teleconferencing and video-taping.

BUYING (AND SELLING) A SMALL BUSINESS
Buying a business is often the easiest way to become an entrepreneur. This book shows how to carefully investigate the potential profitability of a business, how to assess the asking price, and how to be sure you get what you paid for.

FRANCHISING
Buying a franchise can be a good, lower-risk way to go into business for yourself, but it is not an instant road to success. Here is an explanation of royalty terms, franchise sites, and unethical pyramid schemes. Included is a questionnaire to help the buyer identify suitable franchises and practical advice for finding a good investment.

FUNDRAISING FOR NON-PROFIT GROUPS
Raising money is the most essential and also the most difficult task for any organization. This book explains how to do it, from making up the budget to approaching corporation presidents and other possible funders.

GETTING STARTED
If you want to go into business for yourself, either part-time or full-time, you will need to know every sales and marketing tip there is. *Getting Started* offers tips to fight inflation, increase sales, use effective advertising, and increase the success of your business.

LEARN TO TYPE FAST
This book provides a unique method of learning how to type. This new system, which you can learn in five hours, teaches you the keys in relation to your fingers, rather than the keyboard.

A PRACTICAL GUIDE
TO FINANCIAL MANAGEMENT
Practical information for the non-financial manager given with a complete discussion on how to define information needs more clearly, and how to make decisions based on financial information.

NATIONAL TITLES

	Asking Questions	7.95
	Assertiveness for Managers	9.95
	Basic Accounting	6.95
	Be a Better Manager	8.95
	Best Ways to Make Money	5.95
	Better Book for Getting Hired	9.95
	Between the Sexes	8.95
	Business Etiquette Today	7.95
	Business Guide to Effective Speaking	6.95
	Business Guide to Profitable Customer Relations	
	Business Writing Workbook	9.95
	Buying and Selling a Small Business	6.95
	Civil Rights	8.95
	Complete Guide to Home Contracting	19.95
	Credit, Debt, and Bankruptcy	7.95
	Criminal Procedure in Canada	16.95
	Death in the Family	8.95
	Design Your Own Logo	9.95
	Editing Your Newsletter	14.95
	Entrepreneur's Self-Assessment Guide	9.95
	Environmental Law	8.95
	Family Ties That Bind	7.95
	Federal Incorporation and Business Guide	14.95
	Financial Control for the Small Business	6.95
	Financial Freedom on $5 a Day	7.95
	For Sale By Owner	6.95
	Forming and Managing a Non-Profit Organization in Canada	12.95
	Franchising in Canada	6.95
	Fundraising	5.50
	Getting Elected	8.95
	Getting Started	10.95
	How to Advertise	7.95
	How You Too Can Make a Million in the Mail Order Busiess	9.95
	Immigrating to Canada	14.95
	Immigrating to the U.S.A.	14.95
	Keyboarding for Kids	7.95
	Landlording in Canada	14.95
	Learn to Type Fast	11.50
	Managing Stress	7.95
	Marketing Your Product	12.95
	Marketing Your Service	12.95
	Media Law Handbook	6.50
	Medical Law Handbook	6.95
	Mike Grenby's Tax Tips	6.95
	Mobile Retirement Handbook	9.95
	Mortgages & Foreclosure	7.95
	A Nanny For Your Child	7.95
	Newcomer's Guide to the U.S.A.	12.95
	Parent's Guide to Understanding Teenagers and Suicide	
	Patent Your Own Invention	21.95
	Planning for Financial Independence	11.95
	Practical Guide to Financial Management	6.95
	Practical Time Management	6.95
	Radio Documentary Handbook	8.95
	Ready-to-Use Business Forms	9.95
	Retirement Guide for Canadians	9.95
	Selling Strategies for Service Businesses	
	Small Business Guide to Employee Selection	6.95
	Sport and Recreation Law in Canada	
	Start and Run a Profitable Beauty Salon	14.95
	Start and Run a Profitable Consulting Business	12.95
	Start and Run a Profitable Craft Business	10.95
	Start and Run a Profitable Restaurant	10.95
	Start and Run a Profitable Retail Business	11.95
	Starting a Successful Business in Canada	12.95
	Step-Parent Adoptions	12.95
	Taking Care	7.95
	Upper Left-Hand Corner	10.95
	Working Couples	5.50
	Write Right!	5.50

PROVINCIAL TITLES

Divorce Guide
❑ B.C. 9.95 ❑ Alberta 9.95 ❑ Saskatchewan 12.95
❑ Manitoba 11.95 ❑ Ontario 12.95

Employer/Employee Rights
❑ B.C. 7.95 ❑ Alberta 6.95 ❑ Ontario 6.95

Incorporation Guide
❑ B.C. 14.95 ❑ Alberta 14.95 ❑ Manitoba/Saskatchewan 12.95 ❑ Ontario 14.95

Landlord/Tenant Rights
❑ B.C. 7.95 ❑ Alberta 6.95 ❑ Ontario 7.95

Marriage & Family Law
❑ B.C. 7.95 ❑ Alberta 8.95 ❑ Ontario 7.95

Probate Guide
❑ B.C. 12.95 ❑ Alberta 10.95 ❑ Ontario 11.95

Real Estate Guide
❑ B.C. 8.95 ❑ Alberta 7.95 ❑ Ontario 8.50

Small Claims Court Guide
❑ B.C. 7.95 ❑ Alberta 7.50 ❑ Ontario 7.50

Wills
❑ B.C. 6.50 ❑ Alberta 6.50 ❑ Ontario 5.95
❑ Wills/Probate Procedure for Manitoba/Saskatchewan 5.95

PACKAGED FORMS

Divorce Forms
❑ B.C 11.95 ❑ Alberta 10.95 ❑ Saskatchewan 12.95
❑ Manitoba 10.95 ❑ Ontario 14.95

Incorporation
❑ B.C 12.95 ❑ Alberta 14.95 ❑ Saskatchewan 14.95
❑ Manitoba 14.95 ❑ Ontario 14.95 ❑ Federal 7.95
❑ Minute Books 17.95
❑ Power of Attorney Kit 9.95

Probate
❑ B.C. Administration 14.95 ❑ B.C. Probate 14.95
❑ Alberta 14.95 ❑ Ontario 15.50

❑ Rental Form Kit (B.C., Alberta, Saskatchewan, Ontario) 4.95

❑ Have You Made Your Will? 5.95

❑ If You Love Me Put It In Writing — Contract Kit 14.95

❑ If You Leave Me Put It In Writing — B.C. Separation Agreement Kit 14.95

Interim Agreement
❑ B.C. 2.50 ❑ Alberta 2.50 ❑ Ontario 2.50

Note: All prices subject to change without notice.

Books are available in book and department stores, or use the order form below.
Please enclose cheque or money order (plus sales tax where applicable) or give
us your MasterCard or Visa number (please include validation and expiry dates).

(PLEASE PRINT)

Name _____

Address _____

City _____ Province _____

Postal Code _____

❑ Visa/ ❑ MasterCard Number_____

Validation Date_____ Expiry Date _____

If order is under $20.00, add $1.00 for postage and handling.
Please send orders to:
SELF-COUNSEL PRESS
1481 Charlotte Road
North Vancouver, British Columbia V7J 1H1

❑ Check here for free catalogue.

AMERICAN
ORDER FORM
SELF-COUNSEL SERIES   06/88

NATIONAL TITLES

_____	Word Processing	. . . . .8.95
_____	Working Couples	. . . . .5.50

STATE TITLES — WASHINGTON AND OREGON
(Please indicate which state edition is required)

Divorce Guide
        ❏ Washington (with forms) 14.95 ❏ Oregon 11.95
Employer/Employee Rights
        ❏ Washington 5.50
Incorporation and Business Guide
        ❏ Washington 12.95 ❏ Oregon 11.95
Landlord/Tenant Rights
        ❏ Washington 6.95 ❏ Oregon 6.95
Marriage & Family Law
        ❏ Washington 7.95 ❏ Oregon 4.95
Probate Guide
        ❏ Washington 9.95
Real Estate Buying/Selling Guide
        ❏ Washington 6.95 ❏ Oregon 3.95
Small Claims Court Guide
        ❏ Washington 4.50
Wills
        ❏ Washington 6.95 ❏ Oregon 6.95

PACKAGED FORMS

Divorce
        ❏ Oregon Set A (Petitioner) 14.95
        ❏ Oregon Set B (Co-petitioners) 12.95
❏ If You Love Me — Put It In Writing 7.95
Incorporation
        ❏ Washington 12.95 Oregon 12.95
Probate
        ❏ Washington 9.95
Rental Form Kit 3.95
Will and Estate Planning Kit 4.95

All prices subject to change without notice.

_____

(PLEASE PRINT)

NAME_____

ADDRESS _____

CITY_____

STATE _____

ZIP CODE _____

Check or money order enclosed

If order is under $20, add $1.50 for postage and handling
Washington residents add 8.1% sales tax.
Please send orders to:

SELF-COUNSEL PRESS INC.
1303 N. Northgate Way
Seattle, Washington, 98133

❏ Check here for free catalog